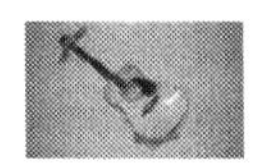

THE ITINERARIUM

OF

DR. ALEXANDER HAMILTON

Written by

Gentleman Alexander Hamilton
(1744)

With an Introduction

by

Atidem Aroha

(Edition 2014)

ISBN-13: 978-1490958521
ISBN-10: 1490958525

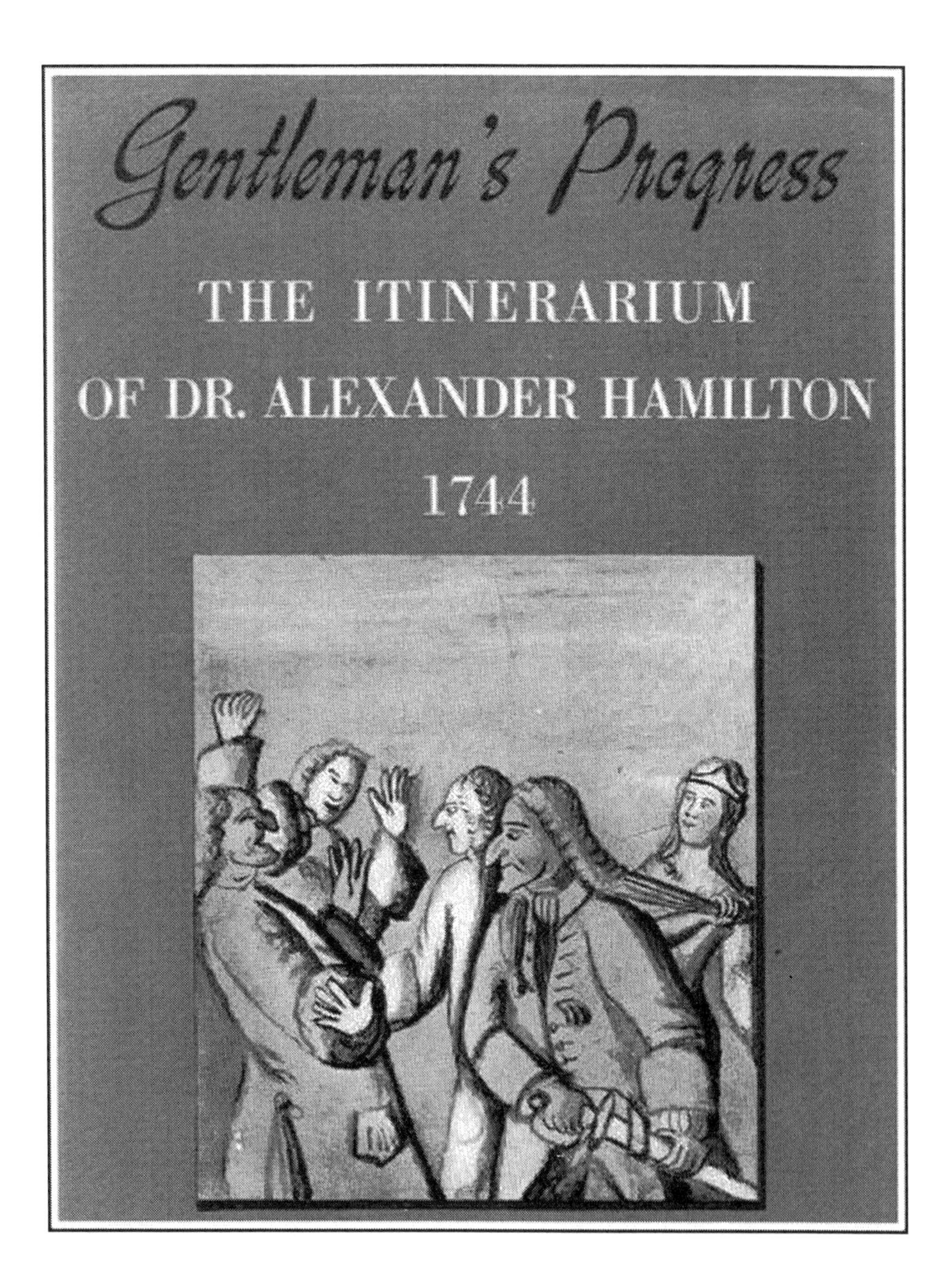
Gentleman's Progress
THE ITINERARIUM
OF DR. ALEXANDER HAMILTON
1744

The Itinerarium of Dr. Alexander Hamilton, 1744.
Gentleman's Progress
The Itinerarium of Dr. Alexander Hamilton, 1744.
Gentleman's Progress
Barcode Area
We will add the barcode for you.
Made with Cover Creator

INTRODUCTION

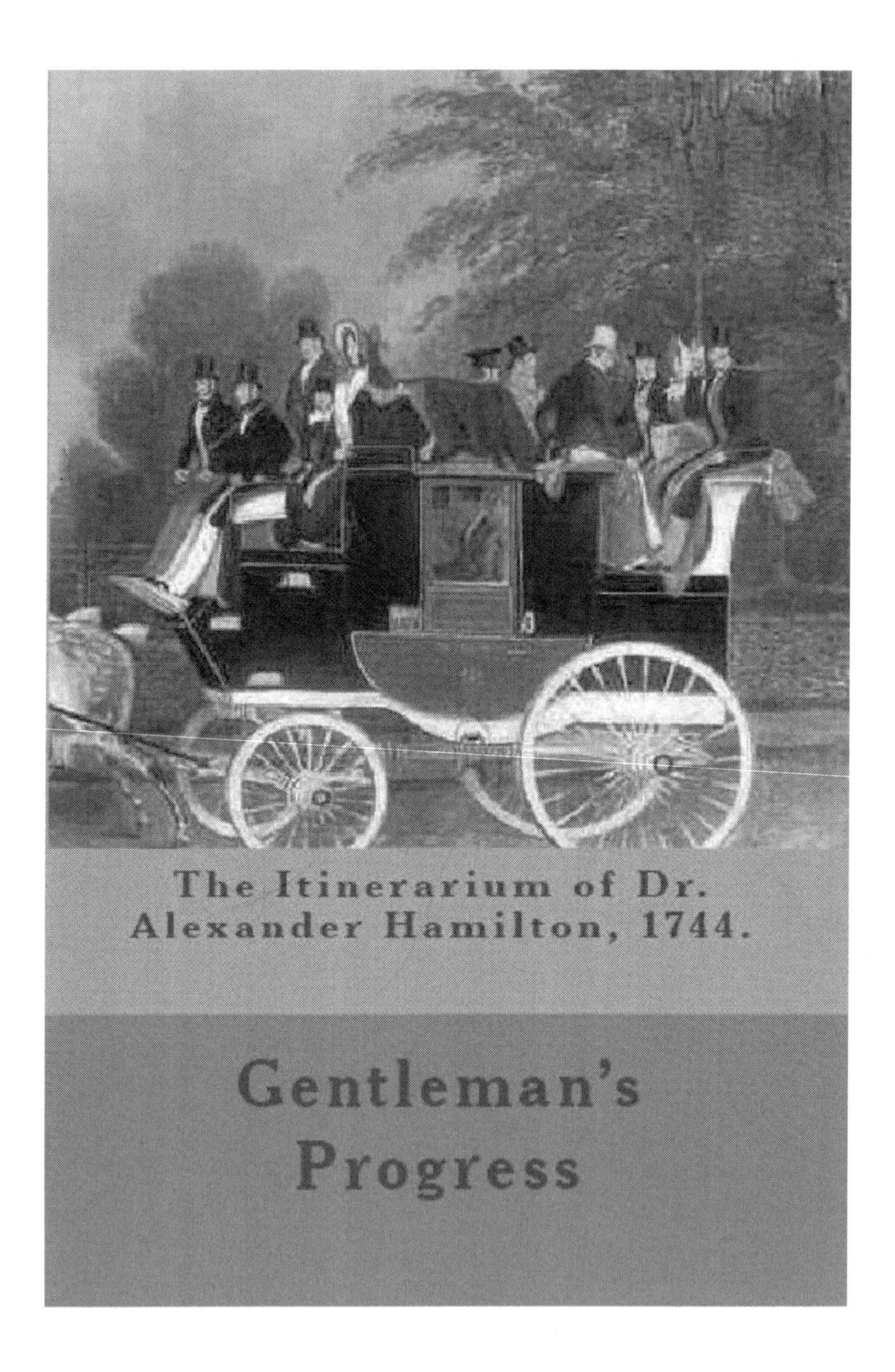
The Itinerarium of Dr.
Alexander Hamilton, 1744.
Gentleman's
Progress

GENTLEMAN'S PROGRESS

Alexander Hamilton was born in Edinburgh, Scotland; graduated in 1737 from medical school and immigrated to Maryland in 1739.[i] During this time colonial America was an evolving society. The Itinerarium of Dr. Alexander Hamilton is a primary source from which we gain insight to the societies and towns that formed the new English colonies in America around the 1740s.

Dr. Hamilton joined his brother John, also a physician, in Maryland where he lived since 1720. He settled in Annapolis, where he became popular. Being a doctor did not prevent him from suffering of tuberculosis, which lead him to think that he would never get married. As a bachelor he embarked in a four month tour totaling 1,624 miles departing from Annapolis, visiting Maryland, Portsmouth, and New Hampshire. Dr. Hamilton travels take us to that life in the New England society of the mid eighteenth century.

We are transported here to the societies of Colonial North America, settled in small towns made up of brick and wood houses and churches. Each church was of a different denomination. In the town's center the clock of the main building remind us those slow motion movies depicting daily European life inhabited by ordinary people. Hamilton encounters different types of personalities in his travels, like the reverent Mr. Dean who advocated against the attempt to reduce the number of taxables, reminding him of the proverb "the shirt is nearest the skin. Touch a man in his private interest, and you immediately procure his ill will.[ii]"

Private interests were of utmost importance during the rapid growth of the New England colonies. The Ohio Valley and the westward rush expansion brought unforeseen problems, mainly because the rush to acquire new land outnumbered the supply. This was an evolving society, where communication networks and newspapers were part of the culture, spreading through the massive influence of outside spectators during the Great Awakening.[iii]

Throughout the narrative we perceive the impact of Whitefield's Awakening message around the northern towns inclining people's religious beliefs to either side of the social spectrum, what Hamilton called the "new light bigots,"[iv] referring to those which take the preached word almost to heart. This Awakening message pushed people outside of institutional structures, infusing a new popular rhetoric very emotional and extemporaneous.[v] Throughout his itinerary, Hamilton dined and traveled with a diverse group of people describing for us the customs of some of these particular towns: Scots, English, Dutch, Germans, Irish, Roman Catholics, Churchmen, Presbyterians, Quakers, Newlightmen, Methodist, Seventh day men, Moravians and Anabaptists[vi].

The towns, at the time, were connected through a network inclusive of post offices, newspapers, and maritime transportation. We learned about towns like Amboy[vii] which was older than the city of New York, or Muman's Island[viii], which had a small nation of Mochacander Indians. The way people used to live and behave, much to our surprise, have similarities even 200 years later, such as the citizenry of New York: "The people of New York at the first appearance of a stranger are seemingly civil and courteous, but this civility and complaisance soon relaxes if he be not either highly recommended or a good toaper.[ix]" As we can see, news and oral communication were a common thread, and rumor of war, as it does today, moved by word of mouth.

The French-Indian War was about to explode and in almost every town this wind presaging a violence to come was felt; a spiritual awakening did not seem enough. French and English were in perpetual competition[x], and because of the necessity of land and the imminent westward movement of the New England colonies, tension was accumulating; the outcome was the confrontation of the English against the French and Indians in some sort of confederation. George Washington had the first shot. Traveling was a dangerous adventure at the time.

While traveling from town to town, and listening to these rumors, Mr. Hamilton used a letter of recommendation as a good passport to be welcomed in different places. The roads at that time were dangerous, thus many people refrained from travel. This apparently was a very serious matter because Alexander met people that did not know where Maryland was nor of its existence. Some towns where strictly constituted by inhabitants from only one nation as Ransbeck, a German town. In Kingstown[xi] he recounts the encounter between a Jew named Abraham Dubois, French by birth, and his dispute with another Englishman about sacred history, particularly the Old Testament; giving us an insight of the importance of religion at that particular time.

Marblehead, a fishing town, had about 5,000 inhabitants but that was not the common case.[xii] Each of these cities and settlements, in 1770, had a population inferior to 2,500 people, representing 93% of the colonies; and only towns like the north port cities of Boston, New York, and Philadelphia among others were able to develop trade and manufacturing, as New England which became the slave port in North America[xiii] acting as big cities for that period of time with a significant influence.

The influence of the European Enlightment was immense, even in America. New ideas, the printing press, the numerous industrial advances, and the steam machines, were mobilizing many to meet in public places and talk about what the present and future held for them in the horizon. Hamilton was enlightened with appreciation; however, he spent time observing other people's behaviors.

Dr. Hamilton is here very hypocritical and intellectually elitist[xiv] For him it seems nobody was good enough, but himself: "A Pennsylvanian will tell a lye with a sanctified, solemn face; a Marylander, perhaps, will convey his fib in a volley of oaths; but the effect and point of view is the same tho' the manner of operating be different"; as in other parts when he 'burnt' ink, paper, and time just criticizing the different personalities that he met in his journey. Dr. Hamilton's narrative gives us first hand information about the culture, daily life, fears, and the hopes of that generation in particular, which is a grain of sand in what we call American History.

Best Regards,
Atidem Aroha
(Editor)

[We have kept the narrative and Itinerarium as originally written]

The Gentleman

Dr. Alexander Hamilton

(Full Text. Original version)

ITINERARIUM
DIE MERCURII TRIGESSIMO MENSIS MAII INCHOATUM ANNO MDCCXLIV

Annapolis, Wednesday, May 30th.–I set out from *Annapolis* in *Maryland*, upon Wednesday the 30th of May at eleven o'clock in the morning; contrary winds and bad weather prevented my intended passage over Chesapeak Bay; so taking the Patapscoe road, I proposed going by the way of Bohemia to Newtown upon Chester, a very circumflex course, but as the journey was intended only for health and recreation, I was indifferent whether I took the nearest or the farthest route, having likewise a desire to see that part of the country. I was in seeming bad order at my first setting out, being suspicious that one of my horses was lame; but he performed well, and beyond my expectation. I travelled but twenty-six miles this day; there was a cloudy sky, and an appearance of rain. Some miles from town I met Mr. H –t going to Annapolis. He returned with me to his own house, where I was well entertained and had one night's lodging and a country dinner.

Mr. H–l, a gentleman of Barbadoes, with whom I expected to have the pleasure of travelling a good part of my intended journey, had left Annapolis a week or ten days before me, and had appointed to meet me at Philadelphia. He went to Bohemia by water, and then took chaise over land to Newcastle and Wilmington, being forbid for certain physical reasons to travel on horseback. This was a polite and facetious gentleman, and I was sorry that his tedious stay in some places put it out my power to tarry for him; so I was deprived of his conversation the far greatest part of the journey.

Mr. H –l and I, after dinner, drank some punch, and conversed like a couple of virtuosos. His wife had no share in the conversation; he is blessed indeed with a silent woman; but her muteness is owing to a defect in her hearing, that without bawling out to her she cannot understand what is spoken, and therefore not knowing how to make pertinent replies, she chuses to hold her tongue. It is well I have thus accounted for it, else such a character in the sex would appear quite out of nature. At night I writ to Annapolis, and retired to bed at ten o'clock.

Thursday, May 31st–I got up betimes this morning, *pour prendre le frais* , as the French term it, and found it heavy and cloudy, portending rain. At nine o'clock I took my leave of Mr. H–t, his wife and sister, and took horse.

A little before I reached Patapscoe ferry, I was overtaken by a certain captain of a tobacco ship, whose name I know not, nor did I inquire concerning it, lest he should think me impertinent.

PATAPSCOE FERRY

We crossed the ferry together at ten o'clock. He talked inveterately against the clergy, and particularly the Maryland clerks of the holy cloth; but I soon found that he was a prejudiced person, for it seems he had been lately cheated by one of our parsons.

BALTIMORE TOWN-GUNPOWDER FERRY-JOPPA

This man accompanied me to Baltimore Town,' and after I parted with him I had a solitary journey till I came within three miles of Gunpowder Ferry, where I met one Matthew Baker, a horsejockey.

Crossing the ferry I came to Joppa, a village pleasantly situated, and lying close upon the river; there I called at one Brown's, who keeps a good tavern in a large brick house. The landlord was ill with intermitting fevers, and understanding from some one there who knew me, that I professed physick, he asked my advice, which I gave him.

Here I encountered Mr. D–n, the minister of the parish, who (after we had despatched a bowl of *sangaree*) carried me to his house. There passed between him, his wife, and me some odd rambling conversation, which turned chiefly upon politicks. I heard him read with great patience some letters from his correspondents in England, written in a gazette style, which seemed to be an abridgement of the political history of the times and a dissection of the machinations of the French, in their late designs upon Great Britain. This reverend gentleman and his wife seemed to express their indignation, with some zeal, against certain of our St–sm–n and C–rsl at Annapolis, who it seems had opposed the interest of the clergy by attempting to reduce the number of the Taxables. This brought the proverb in my mind, *The shirt is nearest the Skin*. Touch a man in his,private interest, and you immediately procure his ill will.

Leaving Joppa I fell in company with one Captain Waters and with Mr. D gs, a virtuoso in botany. He affected some knowledge in Natural Philosophy, but his learning that way was but superficial.

DESCRIPTION OF THE GENSING

He showed me a print or figure of the *Gensing*, which he told me was to be found in the rich bottoms near Susquehanna. The plant is of one stem or stalk, and jointed. From each joint issues four small branches, at the extremity of each of these is a cinquefoil, or five leaves, somewhat oblong, notched and veined. Upon the top of the stem it bears a bunch of red berries, but I could not learn if it had any apparent flower, the colour of that flower, or at what season of the year it blossomed or bore fruit. I intended, however, to look for it upon the branches of Susquehanna, not that I imagined it of any singular virtue, for I think it has really no more than what may be in the common liquorice root, mixed with an aromatick, or spicy drug, but I had a curiosity to see a thing which has been so famous.

After parting with this company, I put up at one Tradaway's, about ten miles from Joppa. The road here is pretty hilly, stony, and full of a small gravel. I observed some stone, which I thought looked like limestone.

Just as I dismounted at Tradaway's, I found a drunken Club dismissing. Most of them had got upon their horses, and were seated in an oblique situation, deviating much from a perpendicular to the horizontal plane, a posture quite necessary for keeping the center of gravity within its proper base, for the support of the superstructure; hence we deduce the true physical reason why our heads overloaded with liquor become too ponderous for our heels. Their discourse was as oblique as their position: the only thing intelligible in it was oaths and Goddamnes; the rest was an inarticulate sound like Rabelais' frozen words a-thawing, interlaced with hickupings and belchings. I was uneasy till they were gone, and my landlord, seeing me stare, made that trite apology,–That indeed he did not care to have such disorderly fellows come about his house; he was always noted far and near for keeping a quiet house and entertaining only gentlemen or such like; but these were country people, his neighbours, and it was not prudent to disoblige them upon slight occasions. "Alas, sir!" added he, "we that entertain travellers must strive to oblige everybody, for it is our daily bread." While he spoke thus our Bacchanalians finding no more rum in play, rid off helter-skelter, as if the devil had possessed them, every man sitting his horse in a seesaw manner like a bunch of rags tied upon the saddle. I found nothing particular or worth notice in my landlord's character or conversation, only as to his bodily make. He was a fat pursy man, and had large bubbies like a woman. I supped upon fried chickens and bacon, and after supper the conversation turned upon politicks, news, and the dreaded French war; but it was so very lumpish and heavy that it disposed me mightily to sleep. This learned company consisted of the landlord, his overseer and miller, and another greasy-thumbed fellow, who, as I understood, professed physick, and particularly surgery in the drawing of teeth.

He practised upon the housemaid, a dirty piece of lumber, who made such screaming and squawling as made me imagine there was murder going forwards in the house. However, the artist got the tooth out at last, with a great clumsy pair of blacksmith's forceps; and indeed it seemed to require such an instrument, for when he showed it to us it resembled a horsenail more than a tooth.

The miller I found professed musick, and would have tuned his crowd' to us, but unfortunately the two middle strings betwixt the bass and treble were broke. This man told us that he could play by the book.

After having had my fill of this elegant company, I went to bed at ten o'clock. *Friday, June 1 st.*–The sun rose in a clear horizon, and the air in these highlands was for two hours in the morning very cool and refreshing. I breakfasted upon some dirty chocolate, but the best that the house could afford, and took horse about half an hour after six in the morning. For the first thirteen miles the road seemed gravelly and hilly, and the land but indifferent.

SUSQUEHANNA FERRY

When I came near Susquehanna Ferry I looked narrowly in the bottoms for the gensing, but could not discover it. The lower ferry of Susquehanna, which I crossed, is above a mile broad. It is kept by a little old man, whom I found at vittles with his wife and family upon a homely dish of fish, without any kind of sauce. They desired me to eat, but I told them I had no stomach. They had no cloth upon the table, and their mess was in a dirty, deep, wooden dish, which they evacuated with their hands, cramming down skins, scales, and all. They used neither knife, fork, spoon, plate, or napkin, because, I suppose, they had none to use. I looked upon this as a picture of that primitive simplicity practised by our forefathers, long before the mechanic arts had supplied them with instruments for the luxury and elegance of life. I drank some of their cider, which was very good, and crossed the ferry in company with a certain Scots-Irishman, by name Thomas Quiet. The land about Susquehanna is pretty high and woody, and the channel of the river rocky.

Mr. Quiet rid a little scrub bay mare, which he said was sick and ailing, and could not carry him, and therefore he lighted every half mile and ran a couple of miles at a footman's pace, to "spell the poor beast" (as he termed it). He informed me he lived at Monocosy, and had been out three weeks in quest of his creatures (horses), four of which had strayed from his plantation. I condoled his loss, and asked him what his mare's distemper was, resolving to prescribe for her, but all that I could get out of him was that the poor silly beast had choaked herself in eating her oats; so I told him that if she was choaked she was past my art to recover. This fellow I observed had a particular down-hanging look, which made me suspect he was one of our New-light bigots.

I guessed right, for he introduced a discourse concerning Whitefield,1 and enlarged pretty much and with some warmth upon the doctrines of that apostle, speaking much in his praise. I took upon me, in a ludicrous manner, to impugn some of his doctrines, which by degrees put Mr. Quiet in a passion. He told me flatly that I was damned without redemption. I replied that I thought his name and behaviour were very incongruous, and desired him to change it with all speed, for it was very improper that such an angry turbulent mortal as he should be called by the name of Thomas Quiet.

PRINCIPIO IRON WORKS

In the height of this fool's passion, I overtook one Mr. B –r, a proprietor in the iron works there, and, after mutual salutation, the topic of discourse turned from religious controversy to politicks; so putting on a little faster we left this inflamed bigot and his sick mare behind. This gentleman accompanied me to Northeast, and gave me directions as to the road.

I crossed Elk Ferry at three in the afternoon. One of the ferry-men, a young fellow, plied his tongue much faster than his oar. He characterized some of the chief dwellers in the neighbourhood, particularly some young merchants, my countrymen, for whom he had had the honour to stand pimp in their amours. He let me know that he understood some scraps of Latin, and repeated a few hexameter lines out of Lilly's Grammar. He told me of a clever fellow of his name, who had composed a book, for which he would give all the money he was master of to have the pleasure of reading it. I asked him who this namesake of his was. He replied that it was one Terence; and to be sure he must have been an arch dog, for he never knew one of the name but he was remarkable for his parts.

BOHEMIA

Thus entertained I got over the ferry, and rid to Bohemia,' and, calling at the manor-house there, I found nobody at home.

I met here a reverend parson, who was somewhat inquisitive as to where I came from, and the news, but I was not very communicative. I understood afterwards it was parson W –e.

BOHEMIA FERRY

I crossed Bohemia Ferry, and lodged at the ferry house. The landlord's name I cannot remember, but he seemed to be a man of tolerable parts for one in his station. Our conversation ran chiefly upon religion. He gave me a short account of the spirit of enthusiasm that had lately possessed the inhabitants of the forests there, and informed me that it had been a common practice for companies of twenty or thirty hair-brained fanaticks to ride thro' the woods singing of psalms.

I went to bed at nine at night; my landlord, his wife, daughters, and I lay all in one room.

Saturday, June 2nd.–In the morning there was a clear sky overhead, but a foggy horizon, and the wind at south, which presaging heat I set out very early.

SASSAFRAX FERRY

I took the road to Newtown upon Chester Ferry, and crossed Sassafrax Ferry at seven o'clock'in the morning, where I found a great concourse of people, at a fair. The roads here are exceeding good and even, but dusty in the summer, and deep in the winter season. The day proved very hot. I encountered no company, and I went three or four miles out of my way.

NEWTOWN

I reached Newtown at twelve o'clock, and put up at Dougherty's, a publick house there. I was scarce arrived, when I met several of my acquaintance. I dined with Dr. Anderson, and spent the rest of the day in a sauntering manner. The Northern post arrived at night. I read the papers, but found nothing of consequence in them, so after some comical chat with my landlord, I went to bed at eleven o'clock at night.

Sunday, June 3d.–I stayed all this day at Newtown, and breakfasted with Th. Clay, where I met with one W–b, a man of the law,–to appearance a civil, good-natured man, but set up for a kind of connoisseur in many things. I went to visit some friends, and dined at the tavern, where I was entertained by the tricks of a female baboon in the yard. This lady had more attendants and hangers-on at her levee than the best person (of quality as I may say) in town. She was very fond of the compliments and company of the men and boys, but expressed in her gestures an utter aversion at women and girls, especially negroes of that sex,–the lady herself being of a black complexion, yet she did not at all affect her country women.

At night I was treated by Captain Binning, of Boston, with a bowl of lemon punch. He gave me letters for his relations at Boston. While we put about the bowl a deal of comical discourse passed, in which the landlord, a man of a particular talent at telling comic stories, bore the chief part.

Monday, June 4th.–The morning being clear and somewhat cool, I got up before five o'clock, and soon mounted horse. I had a solitary route to Bohemia, and went very much out of my way, by being too particular and nice in observing directions.

SASSAFRAX AND BOHEMIA FERRIES

I reached Mr. Alexander's house on the manor at twelve o'clock. There I stayed and dined and drank tea with Miss C–ey. After some talk and laughter I took my leave at five o'clock, designing 12 miles farther, to one Vanbibber's, that keeps a house upon the Newcastle road; but instead of going there I went out of my way, and lay at one Hollinzs Head of Elk.

There is a great marsh upon the left hand of his house, which I passed in the night, thro' the middle of which runs Elk. The multitude of fireflies glittering in the dark upon the surface of this marsh makes it appear like a great plain scattered over with spangles.

In this part of the country, I found they chiefly cultivated British grain,-as wheat, barley and oats. They raise, too, a great deal of flax, and, in every house here, the women have two or three spinningwheels a-going. The roads up this way are tolerably level, but in some places stony. After a light supper I went to bed at ten o'clock.

PENNSYLVANIA-NEWCASTLE

Tuesday, June 5th.–I took horse a little after five in the morning, and after a solitary ride thro stony, unequal road, where the country people stared at me like sheep when I inquired of them the way, I arrived at Newcastle, upon Delaware, at nine o'clock in ye morning and baited my horses at one Curtis's, at the sign of the Indian King, a good house of entertainment.

This town stands upon stony ground, just upon the water, there being from thence a large prospect eastward, towards the Bay of Delaware and the Province of the Jerseys. The houses are chiefly brick, built after the Dutch model, the town having been originally founded and inhabited by the Dutch, when it belonged to New York government. It consists chiefly of one great street, which makes an elbow at right angles. A great many of the houses are old and crazy. There are in the town two public buildings; viz., a court-house and church.

At Curtis's I met company going to Philadelphia, and was pleased at it, being myself an utter stranger to the roads. This company consisted of three men,–Thomas Howard, Timothy Smith, and William Morison. I treated them with some lemon punch, and desired the favour of their company. They readily granted my request, and stayed some time for me, till I had eat breakfast.

Smith, in his coat and hat, had the appearance of a Quaker, but his discourse was purged of *thee's* and *thou's*, tho' his delivery seemed to be solemn and slow-paced.

Howard was a talkative man, abounding with words and profuse in compliments, which were generally blunt, and came out in an awkward manner. He bestowed much panegyrick upon his own behaviour and conduct. Morison (who, I understood, had been at the Land Office in Annapolis, inquiring about a title he had to some land in Maryland) was a very roughspun, forward, clownish blade, much addicted to swearing, at the same time desirous to pass for a gentleman, notwithstanding which ambition, the conscientiousness of his natural boorishness obliged him frequently to frame ill-timed apologies for his misbehaviour, which he termed frankness and freeness. It was often,–"Damn me, gentlemen, excuse me; I am a plain, honest fellow; all is right down plain–dealing, by God." He was much affronted with the landlady at Curtis's, who, seeing him in a greasy jacket and breeches, and a dirty worsted cap, and withal a heavy, forward, clownish air and behaviour, I suppose took him for some ploughman or carman, and so presented him with some scraps of cold veal for breakfast, he having declared that he could not drink "your damned washy tea." As soon as he saw his mess, he swore, –"Damn him, if it wa'n't out of respect to the gentleman in company" (meaning me) "he would throw her cold scraps out at the window and break her table all to pieces, should it cost him 100 pounds for damages." Then, taking off his worsted nightcap, he pulled a linen one out of his pocket, and clapping it upon his head, –"Now," says he, "I 'm upon the borders of Pennsylvania and must look like a gentleman; t' other was good enough for Maryland, and damn my blood, if ever I come into that rascally Province again if I don't procure a leather jacket, that I may be in a trim to box the saucy jacks there and not run the hazard of tearing my coat." This showed, by the bye, that he paid more regard to his modesty and self–denyal. He then made a transition to politicks, and damned the late Sir R W for a rascal.

We asked him his reasons for cursing Sir R–, but he would give us no other but this,–that he was certainly informed by some very good gentlemen who understood the thing right well, that the said Sir R was a damned rogue, and at the conclusion of each rodomontade he told us that tho' he seemed to be but a plain, homely fellow, yet he would have us know that he was able to afford better than many that went finer; he had good linen in his bags, a pair of silver buckles, silver clasps, and gold sleeve buttons, two Holland shirts and some neat nightcaps, and that his little woman at home drank tea twice a day, and he himself lived very well and expected to live better so soon as that old rogue B –t died, and he could secure a title to his land.

The chief topic of conversation among these three Pennsylvanian dons upon the road, was the insignificancy of the neighbouring Province of Maryland when compared to that of Pennsylvania. They laid out all the advantages of the latter which their bungling judgment could suggest, and displayed all the imperfections and disadvantages of the first. They enlarged upon the immorality, drunkenness, rudeness, and immoderate swearing, so much practised in Maryland, and added that no such vices were to be found in Pennsylvania. I heard this and contradicted it not, because I knew that the first part of the proposition was pretty true.

They next fell upon the goodness of the soil, as far more productive of pasturage and grain. I was silent here likewise, because the first proposition was true, but as to the other relating to grain I doubted the truth of it; but what appeared most comical in their criticisms was their making a merit of the stoniness of the roads. "One may ride," says Howard, "fifty miles in Maryland and not see as many stones upon the roads as in fifty paces of road in Pennsylvania." This I knew to be false, but as I thought there was no advantage in stony roads, I even let them take the honour of it to themselves, and did not contradict them.

At Newcastle, I heard news of Mr. H–l, my intended fellow traveller. They told me he was at Willmington upon Cristin River.

CRISTIN .FERRY–WILMINGTON–BRANDYWINE

We crossed that ferry at twelve o'clock, and saw Wilmington about a mile to the left hand. It is about the largeness of Annapolis, but seemingly more compactly built; the houses all brick. We rid seven miles farther to one Foord's, passing over a toll bridge in bad repair, at a place called Brandy wine. At Foord's we dined and baited our horses. There one Usher, a clergyman, joined our company, a man seemingly of good natural parts and civil behaviour, but not overlearned for the cloth. While dinner was getting ready a certain Philadelphian merchant called on Mr.

Howard and with him we had a dish of swearing and loud talking.

After dinner we fell upon politicks, and the expected French war naturally came in, whence arose a learned dispute in company, which was about settling the meaning of the two words *declaration* and *proclamation*. Mr. Smith asserted that a *proclamation of war* was an improper phrase, and that it ought to be a *declaration of war*; and on the other hand a *proclamation o f peace*. Mr. Morrison affirmed with a bloody oath that there might be such a thing as a *proclamation of a declaration*, and swore heartily that he knew it to be true both by experience and hearsay. They grew very loud upon it as they put about the bowl, and I retired into a corner of the room to laugh a little, handkerchief fashion, pretending to be busied in blowing my nose; so I slurred a laugh with nose–blowing.

At last the parson determined all by a learned definition, to this purpose, that a *proclamation* was a publication of anything by authority and a *declaration* only a simple declaring of anything without any authority at all, but the bare assertion of a certain fact, as if I should declare that such a one was drunk at such a time, or that such a person swore so and so.

This dispute ended, we took our horses and rid moderately, it being excessive hot. I observed the common style of salutation upon the road here was *How d'ye*? and How *is't*?

The people all along the road were making of hay, which being green and piled up in rucks, cast a very sweet and agreeable smell. There are here as fine meadows and pasture grounds as any ever I saw in England. The country here is not hilly, nor are the woods very tall or thick. 48.

The people in general follow farming and have very neat brick dwellinghouses upon their farms. 49.

CHESTER

We passed thro' Chester at seven o'clock at night, where we left Morison, Smith, and Howard; and the parson and I jogged on, intending to reach Derby, a town about nine or ten miles from Chester.

Chester is a pretty neat and large village. Built chiefly of brick, pleasantly situated upon a small river of the same name that discharges itself into Delaware, about half a mile below where the village stands. Over this river is a wooden bridge, built with large rafters and planks in form of an arch. The State–house is a pretty enough building; this put me in mind of Chelsea near London, which it resembles for neatness, but is not near so large.

DERBY

The parson and I arrived at Derby, our restingplace, at half an hour after eight at night. This village stands in a bottom and partly upon the ascent of a hill, which makes it have a dull, melancholy appearance. We put up at a publick house kept by one Thomas, where the landlady looked after everything herself, the landlord being drunk as a lord. The liquor had a very strange effect upon him, having deprived him of the use of his tongue. He sat motionless in a corner, smoaking his pipe, and would have made a pretty good figure upon arras.

We were entertained with an elegant dispute between a young Quaker and the boatswain of a privateer, concerning the lawfulness of using arms against an enemy. The Quaker thee'd and thou'd it thro' the nose to perfection, and the privateer's boatswain swore just like the boatswain of a privateer, but they were so far from settling the point that the Quaker had almost acted contrary to his principles, clenching his fist at his antagonist to strike him for bidding God damn him.

At nine Mr. Usher and I went to bed.

SKUYLKILL FERRY

Wednesday, June 6th.–We mounted horse at five in the morning, crossed Skuylkill Ferry at six, and in half an hour more put up our horses at one Cockburn's at the sign of the Three Tons in Chestnut Street.

PHILADELPHIA

The country round the city of Philadelphia is level and pleasant, having a prospect of the large river of Delaware and the Province of East Jersey upon the other ,side. You have an agreeable view of this river for most of the way betwixt Philadelphia and Newcastle. The plan or platform of the city lies betwixt the two rivers of Delaware and Skuylkill, the streets being layed out in rectangular squares, which makes a regular, uniform plan; but upon that account altogether destitute of variety.

At my entering the city I observed the regularity of the streets, but at the same time the majority of the houses mean and low, and much decayed; the streets in general not paved, very dirty and obstructed with rubbish and lumber, but their frequent building excuses that. The State–house, Assembly house,' the great church' in Second street, and Whitefield's Church, are good buildings.

I observed several comical, grotesque Phizzes in the inn where I put up, which would have afforded variety of hints for a painter of Hogarth's turn. They talked there upon all subjects,–politicks, religion, and trade,–some tolerably well, but most of them ignorantly. I discovered two or three chaps very inquisitive, asking my boy who I was, whence come, and whither bound.

I was shaved by a little finical, humpbacked old barber, who kept dancing round me and talking all the time of the operation, and yet did his job lightly and to a hair. He abounded in compliments, and was a very civil fellow in his way. He told me he had been a journeyman to the business for forty odd years, notwithstanding which he understood how to trim gentlemen as well (thank God) as the best masters, and despaired not of preferment before he died.

I delivered my letters, went to dine with Collector Alexander, and visited several people in town. In the afternoon I went to the coffee–house, where I was introduced by Dr. Thomas Bond' to several gentlemen of the place, where the ceremony of shaking of hands, an old custom peculiar to the English, was performed with great gravity, and the usual compliments. I took private lodgings at Mrs. Cume's in Chestnut Street.

Thursday, June 7th.– I remarked one instance of industry as soon as I got up and looked out at my chamber window, and that was the shops open at five in the morning. I breakfasted with Mrs. Cume, and dined by invitation with Dr. Thomas Bond, where after some talk upon physical matters he showed me some pretty good anatomical preparations of the muscles and blood–vessels injected with wax.

After dinner Mr. V–bles, a Barbadian gentleman, came in, who, when we casually had mentioned the freemasons, began to rail bitterly against that society, as an impudent, assuming, and vain cabal, pretending to be wiser than all mankind besides, an *imperium in imperio*, and therefore justly to be discouraged and suppressed, as they had lately been in some foreign countries. Tho' I am no freemason myself, I could not agree with this gentleman, for I abhor all tyrannical and arbitrary notions. I believe the freemasons to be an innocent and harmless society that have in their constitution nothing mysterious or beyond the verge of common human understanding, and their secret, which has made such a noise, I imagine is just no secret at all.

In the evening at the coffee–house, I met Mr. H–l, and inquiring how he did and how he had fared on his way, he replied as to health he was pretty well, but he had almost been devoured with bugs and other vermin, and had met with mean, low company, which had made him very uneasy. He added that he had heard good news from Barbadoes concerning his friends there,–from one, who he imagined called himself Captain *Scrotum*, a strange name indeed, but this gentleman had always some comical turn in his discourse.

I parted with him, and went to the tavern with Mr. Currie and some Scots gentlemen, where we spent the night agreeably, and went home sober at eleven o'clock.

Friday, June 8th.–I read Montaigne's Essays in the forenoon, which is a strange medley of subjects, and particularly entertaining.

I dined at a tavern with a very mixed company of different nations and religions. There were Scots, English, Dutch, Germans, and Irish; there were Roman Catholicks, Churchmen, Presbyterians, Quakers, Newlightmen, Methodists, Seventhdaymen, Moravians, Anabaptists, and one Jew. The whole company consisted of twenty–five, planted round an oblong table, in a great hall well stocked with flies. The company divided into committees in conversation; the prevailing topick was politicks, and conjectures of a French war. A knot of Quakers there talked only about selling of flour and the low price it bore; they touched a little upon religion, and high words arose among some of the sectaries, but their blood was not hot enough to quarrel, or, to speak in the canting phrase, their zeal wanted fervency. of questions concerning Maryland, understanding I had come from thence. In my replies I was reserved, pretending to know little of the matter, as being a person whose business did not lie in the way of history and politicks.

In the afternoon I went to see some ships that lay in the river. Among the rest were three vessels a–fitting out for privateers,–a ship, a sloop, and a schooner. The ship was a large vessel, very high and full–rigged; one Captain Mackey intended to command her upon the cruise. At six o'clock I went to the coffee–house and drank a dish of coffee with Mr. H–l.

After staying there an hour or two, I was introduced by Dr. Phineas Bond into the Governour's Club, a society of gentlemen that meet at a tavern every night, and converse on various subjects. The Governour gives them his presence once a week, which is generally upon Wednesday, so that I did not see him there. Our conversation was entertaining; the subject was the English poets and some of the foreign writers, particularly Cervantes, author of Don Quixote, whom we loaded with eulogiums due to his character.

At eleven o'clock I left this club and went to my lodging.

Saturday, June 9th.–This morning there fell a light rain, which proved very refreshing, the weather having been very hot and dry for several days. he heat in this city is excessive, the sun's rays eing reflected with such power from the brick houses, and from the street pavement, which is brick; the people commonly use awnings of painted cloth or duck over their shop doors and windows, and at sunset throw bucketsful of water upon the pavement, which gives a sensible cool. They are stocked with plenty of excellent water in this city, there being a pump at almost every fifty paces' distance.

There are a great number of balconies to their houses, where sometimes the men sit in a cool habit and smoke.

The market in this city is perhaps the largest in North America. It is kept twice a week, upon Wednesdays and Saturdays. The street where it stands, called Market Street, is large and spacious, composed of the best houses in the city.

They have but one publick clock here, which strikes the hour, but has neither index nor dialplate. It is strange they should want such an ornament and conveniency in so large a place, but the chief part of the community consisting of Quakers they would seem to shun ornament in their publick edifices as well as in their apparel or dress.

The Quakers here have two large meetings;' the Church of England one great church in Second Street, and another built for Whitefield, in which one Tennent, a fanatic, now preaches; the Romans one chapel; the Anabaptists one or two meetings, and the Presbyterians two.

The Quakers are the richest and the people of greatest interest in this government; of them their ouse of Assembly is chiefly composed. They have the character of an obstinate stiff–necked generation, and a perpetual plague to their Governours. The present Governour, Mr. Thomas, has fallen upon a way to manage them better than any of his predecessors did, and at the same time keep pretty much in their good graces, and share some of their Favours.

However, the standing or falling of the Quakers in the House of Assembly depends upon their making sure the interest of the Palatines in this Province, who of late have turned so numerous that they can sway the votes which way they please.

Here is no publick magazine of arms, nor any method of defence either for city or Province in case of the invasion of an enemy; this is owing to the obstinacy of the Quakers in maintaining their principle of non–resistance. It were pity but they were put to a sharp trial to see whether they would act as they profess.

I never was in a place so populous where the gout for publick gay diversions prevailed so little. There is no such thing as assemblies of the gentry among them, either for dancing or musick; these they have had an utter aversion to ever since Whitefield preached among them. Their chief employ, indeed, is traffick and mercantile business, which turns their thoughts from these levities. Some Virginia gentlemen that came here with the Commissioners of the Indian treaty were desirous of having a ball, but could find none of the female sex in a humour for it. Strange influence of religious enthusiasm upon human nature to excite an aversion at these innocent amusements for the most part so agreeable and entertaining to the young and gay, and indeed, in the opinion of moderate people, so conducive to the improvement of politeness, good manners, and humanity.

I was visited this morning by an acquaintance from Annapolis, of whom inquiring the news, I could not learn anything material.

I dined at the tavern, and, returning home after dinner, I read part of a book lately writ by Fielding, entitled *The Adventures o f Joseph Andrews*, a masterly performance of its kind, and entertaining; the characters of low life here are naturally delineated, and the whole performance is so good that I have not seen anything of that kind equal or excel it.

This proved a rainy afternoon, which, because it abated the sultry heat, was agreeable. I drank tea with Collector Alexander, where I saw Mr. H–l.

Their conversation turned upon the people in Barbadoes, and as I knew nothing of the private history of that island, I only sat and heard, for they went upon nothing but private characters and persons. This is a trespass on good manners which many well–bred people fall into thro' inadvertency, two engrossing all the conversation upon a subject which is strange and unknown to a third person there.

At six in the evening I went to my lodging, and looking out at the window, having been led there by a noise in the street, I was entertained by a boxing match between a master and his servant. The master was an unwieldy, pot–gutted fellow, the servant muscular, raw–boned, and tall; therefore tho' he was his servant in station of life, yet he would have been his master in single combat, had not the bystanders assisted the master and holp him up as often as the fellow threw him down. The servant by his dialect was a Scotsman; the names he gave his master were no better than "little bastard," .... terms ill applied to such a pursy load of flesh.

This night proved very rainy.

Sunday, June 10th.–This proved a very wet morning, and there was a strange and surprising alteration of the temperature of the air, from hot and dry (to speak in the style of that elegant and learned physician, Dr. Salmon, and some other ancient philosophers) to cold and moist.

I intended to have gone to church or meeting to edify by the Word, but was diverted from my good purpose by some polite company I fell into, who were all utter strangers to churches and meetings. But I understood that my negro Dromo very piously stepped into the Lutheran Church to be edified with a sermon preached in High Dutch, which, I believe, when dressed up in the fashion of a discourse, he understood every bit as well as English, and so might edify as much with the one as he could have done with the other.

I dined at a private house with some of my countrymen, but our table chat was so trivial and trifling that I mention it not. After dinner I read the second volume of The Adventures o f *Joseph Andrews*, and thought my time well spent.

I drank tea with Mrs. Cume at 5 o'clock. There was a lady with her who gave us an elegant dish of scandal to relish our tea. At six o'clock I went to the coffee–house, where I saw the same faces I had seen before. This day we had expresses from New York, which brought instructions to proclaim war against France, and there was an express immediately despatched to Annapolis in Maryland for the same purpose.

Monday, June 11th.–The morning proved clear, and the air cool and refreshing, which was a great relaxation and relief after the hot weather that had preceded. I read Montaigne's *Essays* in the morning, and was visited by Dr. Lloyd Zachary,' a physician in this place.

I dined with Collector Alexander, and went in the afternoon in the company of some gentlemen to attend the Governour to the Court–house stairs, where war was publickly to be proclaimed against France.

There were about two hundred gentlemen attended Governour Thomas. Col. Lee, of Virginia, walked at his right hand, and Secretary Peters' upon his left; the procession was led by about thirty flags and ensigns taken from privateer vessels and others in the harbour, which were carried by a parcel of roaring sailors. They were followed by eight or ten drums that made a confounded martial noise, but all the instrumental music they had was a pitiful scraping negro fiddle, which followed the drums, and could not be heard for the noise and clamour of the people and the rattle of the drums. There was a rabble of about 4,000 people in the street, and great numbers of ladies and gentlemen in the windows and balconies. Three proclamations were read,–ist, the King of England's proclamation of war against the French King; and, a proclamation for the encouragement of such as should fit out privateers against the enemy; 3d, the Governour of Pennsylvania's proclamation for that Province in particular, denouncing war and hostility against France.

When Secretary Peters had read these, the Governour with a very audible voice "desired all such persons as were fit to carry arms to provide themselves, every man with a good musket, cartouche box, powder and shot, and such implements as were requisite either to repel or annoy the enemy, if there should be any necessity or occasion," adding that he should surely call upon each of them to see that they were provided, "for depend upon it," says he, "this Province shall not be lost by any neglect or oversight of mine."

The Governour having thus spoke, a certain bold fellow in the crowd with a stentorian voice made this reply,–"Please your Honour," says he, "what you say is right, but I and many others here, poor men, have neither money nor credit to procure a musket or the third part of a musket, so that unless the publick takes care to provide us, the bulk of the people must go unfurnished, and the country be destitute of defence." The Governour made no reply, but smiled; so went into his chariot with Col. Lee and the Secretary, and drove homewards.

In the evening I drank tea with Mrs. Cume and went to the coffee–house. At seven o'clock I went to the Governour's Club, where were a good many strangers. Among the rest Captain Mackay, commander of the privateer ship. The conversation ran chiefly upon trade, and the late expedition at Cartagene. Several toasts were drank, among which were some celebrated ones of the female sex.

Tuesday, June 12th.–This seemed to me an idle kind of a day, and the heat began to return. I prepared my baggage, intending to–morrow to proceed c)n my journey towards New York, which city I proposed to be my next resting–place. I breakfasted abroad, and dined at the tavern, where I met anDther strange medley of company, and among the rest a trader from Jamaica, a man of an inquisitive disposition, who seized me for half an hour, but I was upon the reserve.

I drank tea with Mrs. Cume at five o'clock. There was with her a masculine–faced lady, very much pitted with the smallpox. I soon found she was a Presbyterian, and a strait–laced one too. She discovered my religion before I spoke. "You, sir," said she, "were educated a Presbyterian, and I hope you are not like most of your countrymen of that persuasion, who when they come abroad in the world shamefully leave the meeting and go to Church." I told her that I had dealt impartially betwixt both since I came to the place, for I had gone to neither. "That is still worse," said she.

I found this lady pretty well versed in the church history of Maryland. "I am surprised," said she, "how your government can suffer such a rascally clergy. Maryland. has become a receptacle, and, as it were, a common shore for all the filth and scum of that order. I am informed that tailors, cobblers, blacksmiths, and such fellows, when they cannot live like gentlemen by their trades in that place go home to take orders of some latitudinarian bishop, and return learned preachers, setting up for teachers of the people, that have more need of schooling themselves, but that might bear some excuse if their lives were exemplary and their morals good; but many of them are more compleatly wicked than the most profligate and meanest of the laity. It is a shame that such fellows should be inducted into good livings, without any further ceremony or inquiry about them than a recommendation from L–d B–re.

"The English think fit sometimes to be very merry upon the ignorance and stupidity of our Presbyterian clerks. I am sorry indeed that it is too true that many of them have exposed themselves in ridiculous colours, but notwithstanding this can the generality of their clergy, as wise and learned as they are, show such good behaviour and moral life? Besides, generally speaking, in Scotland, where the Presbyterian constitution is the National Church, they admit none now to holy orders who have not had a college education, studied divinity regularly and undergone a thorough examination before a Presbytery of clerks. Do the English do so? No; their inferior clergy are rascally fellows, who have neither had a fit education nor had their knowledge put to the trial by examination; but undergoing some foolish ceremony or farce from a bishop, commence teachers presently, and prove afterwards inferior to none for ignorance and vice. Such are your Maryland clerks."

I heard this long harangue with patience, and attempted to speak in defence of our clergy, but this lady's instructions bore such credit with her that she would not be contradicted. I quoted the maxim of Constantine the Great, who used to say that when a clergyman offended he would cover him with his cloak; but her charity for the order I found did not extend so far, so I allowed her to run on in this kind of critical declamation till her stock was exhausted.

I must make a few remarks before I leave this place. The people in general are inquisitive concerning strangers. If they find one comes there upon the account of trade or traffic, they are fond of dealing with him and cheating him, if they can. If he comes for pleasure or curiosity, they take little or no notice of him, unless he be a person of more than ordinary rank; then they know as well as others how to fawn and cringe.

Some persons there were inquisitive about the state of religion in Maryland. My common reply to such questions was that I studied their constitutions more than their consciences, so knew something of the first, but nothing of the latter.

They have in general a bad notion of the neighbouring Province, Maryland, esteeming the people a set of cunning sharpers; but my notion of the affair is, that the Pennsylvanians are not a whit inferior to them in the science of chicane, only their method of tricking is different. A Pennsylvanian will tell a lie with a sanctified, solemn face; a Marylander perhaps will convey his fib in a volley of oaths; but the effect and point in view are the same, tho' the manner of operating be different.

In this city one may live tolerably cheap, as to the articles of eating and drinking, but European goods here are extravagantly dear. Even goods of their own manufacture–such as linen, woolen, and leather–bear a high price. Their government is a kind of anarchy (or no government), there being perpetual jars betwixt the two parts of the legislature, but that is no strange thing, the ambition and avarice of a few men in both parties being the active springs in these dissensions and altercations, tho' a specious story about the good and interest of the country is trumped up by both; yet I would not be so severe as to say so of all in general.

Mr. T–s,' the present Governour, I believe, is an upright man, and has the interest of the Province really at heart, having done more for the good of that obstinate generation, the Quakers, than any of his predecessors have done. Neither are they so blind as not to see it, for he shares more of their respect than any of their former Governours were wont to do.

There is polite conversation here among the better sort, among whom there is no scarcity of men of learning and good sense. The ladies, for the most part, keep at home and seldom appear in the streets, never in publick assemblies, except at the churches or meetings; therefore I cannot with certainty enlarge upon their charms, having had little or no opportunity to see them either congregated or separate, but to be sure the Philadelphia dames are as handsome as their neighbours.

The staple of this Province is bread, flour, and pork. They make no tobacco but a little for their own use. The country is generally plain and level, fruitful in grain and fruits, pretty well watered, and abounding in woods backward; it is upon the growing hand, more than any of the Provinces of America. The Germans and High Dutch are of late become very numerous here.

Wednesday, June 13th.–Early in the morning I set out from Philadelphia, being willing to depart that city, where upon account of the excessive heat it was a pain to live and breathe. Two gentlemen of the city, Mr. Currie and Mr. Wallace, complimented me with their company five miles of the road. I remarked in the neighbourhood of Philadelphia some stone bridges, the first that I had seen in America. The country people whom I met asked in general whether war had been proclaimed against France.

SHAMANY FERRY, BRISTOL

About nine in the morning I crossed Shamanys Ferry, and half an hour after rested at Bristo', a small town twenty miles northeast of Philadelphia situated upon Delaware River, opposite to which upon the other side of the river stands Burlington, the chief town in the East Jerseys.

I put up my horses in Bristo',1 and breakfasted at Malachi Walton's at the sign of the Crown, intending to tarry till the cool of the evening, and then proceed to Trenton, about ten miles farther.

Bristo' is pleasantly situated, and consists of one street that runs upon a descent towards the river, and then, making an angle or elbow, runs parallel to the river for about a quarter of a mile. Here are some wharfs, pretty commodious for small vessels to load and unload.

The houses in the town are chiefly brick, and the adjacent land pretty level and woody.

DELAWARE FERRY–JERSEY GOVERNMENTTRENTON

I took horse about five in the afternoon, crossed the ferry of Delaware about seven o'clock, and a little after arrived at Trenton in East Jersey.

Upon the left hand, near the river, on the Jersey side, is a pretty box of a house, the property of Governour Thomas of Pennsylvania, in which Colonel Morris,2 the present Governour of the jerseys, lives. Upon the right hand, close upon the town, is a fine water mill, belonging likewise to Colonel Thomas, with a very pretty cascade, that falls over the dam, like a transparent sheet, about thirty yards wide.

I was treated, at my entry into the town, with a dish of staring and gaping from the shop doors and windows, and I observed two or three people laying hold of Dromo's stirrups, inquiring, I suppose, who I was, and whence I came.

I put up at one Eliah Bond's at the sign of the Wheat Sheaf. Two gentlemen of the town came there, and invited me into their company. One was named Cadwaller, a doctor in the place, and, as I understood, a fallen–off Quaker.

We supped upon cold gammon and a salad. Our discourse was mixed and rambling; at first, it was political; then Cadwaller gave me the character of the constitution and government. The House of Assembly here he told me was chiefly composed of mechanics and ignorant wretches, obstinate to the last degree; that there were a number of proprietors in the government and a multitude of Quakers. He enlarged a little in the praise of Governour Morris, who is now a very old man.

From politics the discourse turned to religion and then to physick. Cadwaller asked me concerning several people in Maryland, and among the rest (not yet knowing me) he came across myself, asking me if Hamilton at Annapolis was dead or alive. "Here he is," says I, "bodily and not spiritually."

He told me the reason why he inquired was that about a twelvemonth ago, one Dr. Thomson' from Maryland had been there, and had reported he was going to settle at Annapolis in place of Hamilton there, who they did not expect would live; "but, sir," says he, "if you be the man, I congratulate you upon your unexpected recovery."

Thus passing from one subject to another in discourse, Cadwaller inveighed bitterly against the idle ceremonies that had been foisted into religious worship by almost all sects and persuasions; "not that there was anything material in these ceremonies to cavil at, providing the true design of them was understood, and they were esteemed only as decent decorations and ornaments to divine service in the temples and churches, but upon account that the vulgar in all ages had been misled and imposed upon by wicked, politic, and designing priests and persuaded that the strength and sinews of religion lay in such fopperies, and that there was no such thing as being a good man or attaining salvation without all this trumpery. It is certain," added he, "that a superstitious regard and veneration to the mere ceremonials of religion has contributed very much to corrupt the manners of men, turning their thoughts from true morality and virtue (to promote which ought to be the sole aim of all religions whatsoever) to dwell upon dreams, chimeras fit only to distract the human mind, and give place for mad zeal, the woeful author of persecution, murder, and cruelty."

To this I replied that "priests of all sorts and sects whatsoever made a kind of trade of religion, contriving how to make it turn out to their own gain and profit, yet notwithstanding many were of opinion that to inculcate religion into vulgar minds we must use other methods than only preaching up fine sense and morality to them. Their understanding and comprehension are too gross and thick to receive it in that shape. Men of sense of every persuasion whatsoever are sensible of the emptiness and nonsense of the mere ceremonial part of religion, but at the same time allow it to be in some degree necessary and useful, because the ignorant vulgar are to be dealt with in this point as we manage children by showing them toys in order to persuade them to do that which all the good reasoning of the world never would. The mobile, that many headed beast, cannot be reasoned into religious and pious duties. Men are not all philosophers, the tools by which we must work upon the gross senses and rough–cast minds of the vulgar are such as form and lay before their eyes rewards and punishments, whereby the passions of hope and fear are excited; and withal our doctrines must be interlaced with something amazing and mysterious in order to command their attention, strengthen their belief, and raise their admiration, for was one to make religion appear to them in her genuine, simple, and plain dress, she would gain no credit and would never be regarded."

Here Cadwaller interrupted me and said "all these discourses signified nothing, for he thought she was very little regarded even as it was."

We dismissed at twelve at night.

Thursday, June 14th.–A little after five in the morning I departed Trenton, and rid twelve miles of a very pleasant road, well stored with houses of entertainment.

The country round about displays variety of agreeable prospects and rural scenes. I observed many large fields of wheat, barley, and hemp, which is a great staple and commodity now in this Province; but very little maize, or Indian corn,–only two or three small fields I observed in riding about forty miles. They plant it here much thicker than in Maryland, the distance of one stalk from another not exceeding two feet and a half or three feet at most.

All round you in this part of the country you observe a great many pleasant fertile meadows and pastures, which diffuse at this season of the year, in the cool of the morning, a sweet and refreshing smell. The houses upon the road are many of them built with rough stone.

PRINCETOWN

I passed thro' Princetown, a small village, at eight in the morning, and was saluted with How' st ni tar by an Indian traveller. About half a mile from this village I observed upon the road a quarry of what appeared to me gray slate, the first I had seen in America.

KINGSTON

AT half an hour after eight in the morning, I put up at one Leonard's at the sign of the Black Lion in Kingstown, another small village upon the road. I breakfasted there upon a dish of tea, and was served by a pretty smiling girl, the landlord's daughter. After breakfast, as I sat in the porch, there arrived a waggon with some company. There were in it two Irishmen, a Scotsman, and a Jew. The .Jew's name was Abraham Dubois, a Frenchman by birth. He spoke such bad English that I could scarce understand him. Ile told me he had been at Conestogo to visit some relations he had there; that he left that place upon Monday last, and at that time there had arrived there forty canoes of Indians of the tribes of the Mohooksl and Five Nations, going to treat with the Governours and Commissioners of the American Provinces. This Jew and the company that were with him began a dispute about sacred history. He insisted much upon the books of Moses and the authority of the Old

Testament. He asked the Scotsman, in particular, if he believed the Old Testament. He replied that "nowadays there were few Old Testament people, all having become Newlightmen; for," says he, "among the Christians, one wife is sufficient for one man, but your Old Testament fornicators were allowed a plurality of wives and as many concubines as they could afford to maintain." The Jew made no answer to this nonsensical reply, but began very wisely to settle what day of the week it was, and what time of that day, that God began the creation of the world. He asserted that "It was upon the day that the Christians call Sunday, and that when the light first appeared it was in the west, and therefore it was in the evening that the creation was begun." "Had that evening no morning then?" replied the Scotsman with a sneer. To which the Jew answered that there had been no dawn or sunrising that day, because the sun was not yet created, to run his diurnal course, but that a glorious stream of light suddenly appeared by the mandate of God in the west." "I never heard of an evening without a morning in my life before," replied his antagonist, "and it is nonsense to suppose any such thing." "Cannot black exist," said the Jew, "without its opposite white?" "It may be so," said the Scotsman, "but why does your countryman Moses say and the evening and the morning was the first day?'" The Jew answered that the evening was there first mentioned, because the work was begun upon the evening, at which the Scotsman swore that the words were misplaced by the translators, which pert reply put an end to the dispute. After a deal of such stuff about the Jewish sabbath and such like subjects, the waggon and company departed. They travel here in light convenient waggons, made somewhat chaise–fashion, being high behind and low before, many of them running upon four wheels, so that the horses bear no weight, but only draw, and by this means they can travel at a great rate, perhaps forty or fifty miles a day. Betwixt twelve o'clock and three in the afternoon, there came up three smart thunder gusts, with which fell a deal of rain, but it did not much cool the air. In the middle of the first rain a solemn old fellow lighted at the door. He was in a homely rustic dress, and I understood his name was Morgan. "Look ye here," says the landlord to me, "here comes a famous philosopher.–Your servant, Mr. Morgan, how d'ye?" The old fellow had not settled himself long upon his seat, before he entered upon a learned discourse concerning astrology and the influences of the stars, in which he seemed to put a great deal more confidence than I thought was requisite. From that he made a transition to the causes of the tides, the shape and dimensions of the earth, the laws of gravitation and fifty other physical subjects, in which he seemed to me not to talk so much out of the way as he did upon the subject of judicial astrology. At every period of this old philosopher's discourse, the landlord's address to him was, "Pray, Mr. Morgan, you that are a philosopher, know such and such reasons for such and such things, please inform the gentleman of your opinion." Then he fell upon physick, and told us that he was a–riding for his health. I found him very deficient in his knowledge that way, tho' a great pretender. All this chat passed while the old fellow drank half a pint of wine, which done, the old don took to his horse and rid off in a very slow solemn pace, seemingly well satisfied with his own learning and knowledge. When he was gone inquired of the landlord more particularly concerning him, who told me that he was the most conspicuous and notorious philosopher in all these American parts; that he understood "mademadigs" [mathematics] to a hair's breadth, and had almost discovered whereabouts the longitude lay, and had writ home to the States of Holland and some other great folks about it, a great while ago, but had as yet received no answer. A little after two o'clock we went to dinner, and at four I took horse, having in company a comical old fellow named Brown, that was going to New York to examine the old records concerning some land he had a title to in the lower counties of Pennsylvania government. This old fellow entertained me the whole way with points of law, and showed himself tolerably well versed for one of his education, in the quirps, quibbles, and the roguish part of that science. As we jogged on I observed some mountanous land about 15 or 16 miles to the northward.

BRUNSWICK

WE arrived at six o'clock at Brunswick, a neat small city in East Jersey government, built chiefly of brick and lying upon Raritan River, about sixty miles northeast of Philadelphia. I put up this night at one Miller's, at the sign of Admiral Vernon, and supped with some Dutchmen and a mixed company of others. I had a visit from one Dr. Farquhar in town, who did not stay long with me, being bound that night for New York by water. Our conversation at supper was such a confused medley that I could make nothing of it. I retired to bed at eleven o'clock, after having eat some very fine pickled oysters for supper.

RARITAN FERRY

Friday, June 15th.–A little before six in the morning I forded Raritan River. The tide being low and the scow aground, so that I could not ferry it over, I went by the way of Perth Amboy, but before I came to that place I was overtaken by two men, a young man and an old, grave, sedate fellow. The young man gave me the salute, which I returned and told him that, if he was going to Amboy, I should be glad of company.

He replied he was going that way. First of all, as it is natural, we inquired concerning news.

I gave him an account of such scraps of news as I had picked up at Philadelphia, and he gave me an account of a capture that had well–nigh been made of an English sloop by a Frenchman that had the impudence to pursue her into the hook at the entrance of York Bay, but the English vessel, getting into Amboy harbour, the Frenchman betook himself to sea again; "but had this French rogue known Amboy as well as I," added my newsmonger, "he would have taken her there at anchor." After discussing news, we discoursed concerning horses, by which I discovered that my chap was a jockey by trade. the old don spoke not one word all the way, but coughed and chewed tobacco. At nine in the morning we stopped at the sign of the King's Arms in Amboy, where I breakfasted. As I sat in the porch I observed an antique figure pass by, having an old plaid banyan, a pair of thick worsted stockings ungartered, a greasy worsted nightcap, and no hat. "You see that original," said the landlord; "he is an old bachelor, and it is his humour to walk the street always in that dress. Tho' he makes but a pitiful appearance, yet is he proprietor of most of the houses in town. He is very rich, yet for all that has no servant, but milks his own cow, dresses his own vittles, and feeds his own poultry himself." Amboy is a small town. It is a very old American city, being older than the city of New York; being a chartered city, much less than our Annapolis, and here frequently the Supreme Court and Assembly sit. It has in it one Presbyterian meeting, and a pretty large market house, lately built. It is the principal town in New Jersey, and appears to be laid out in the shape of a St. George's cross, one main street cutting the other at right angles. 'T is a seaport, having a good harbour, but small trade.

They have here the best oysters I have eat in America. It lies close upon the water, and the best houses in town are ranged along the water side. In the jerseys the people are chiefly Presbyterians and Quakers, and there are so many proprietors that share the lands in New Jersey and so many doubtful titles and rights, that it creates an inexhaustible and profitable pool for the lawyers.

At ten o'clock I crossed the ferry to Staten Island, where are some miles of pretty stony, sandy, and uneven road.

NEW YORK GOVERNMENT–STATEN ISLAND

I took notice of one entire stone there about ten feet high, twelve feet long, and six or seven feet thick. At one end of it grew an oak–tree, the trunk of which seemed to adhere or grow to the stone. It lay close by a little cottage, which it equalled pretty near in dimensions. I remarked this stone, because I had not seen so large a one anywhere but in the Highlands of Scotland.

A great many of the trees here are hung thick with long hairy gray moss, which if handsomely oiled and powdered and tied behind with a bag or ribbon would make a tolerable beau–periwig. In this island are a great many poor thatched cottages. It is about eighteen miles long and six or seven miles broad. It seers to abound with good pasture, and is inhabited by farmers. There are in or near it some towns, the chief of which are Katharine's Town, Cuckold's Town,' and Woodbridge.

NARROWS FERRY

I came to the Narrows at two o'clock, and dined at one Corson's, that keeps the ferry. The landlady spoke both Dutch and English. I dined upon what I never had eat in my life before,–a dish of fried clams, of which shell fish there is abundance in these parts.

As I sat down to dinner I observed a manner of saying grace quite new to me. My landlady and her two daughters put on solemn, devout faces, hanging down their heads and holding tip their hands for half a minute. I, who had gracelessly fallen to, without remembering that duty, according to a wicked custom I had contracted, sat staring at them, with my mouth chock–full, but after this short meditation was over we began to lay about us and stuff down the fried clams, with rye bread and butter. They took such a deal of chewing that we were long at dinner, and the dish began to cool before we had eat enough.

The landlady called for the bedpan. I could not guess what she intended to do with it, unless it was to warm her bed to go to sleep after dinner; but I found that it was used by sway of a chafing–dish to warm our dish of clams. I stared at the novelty for some time, and reaching over for a mug of beer that stood on the opposite side of the table, my bag sleeve caught hold of the handle of the bedpan, and unfortunately overset the clams, at which the landlady was a little ruffled, and muttered a scrap of Dutch, of which I understood not a word, except i)iynheer, but I suppose she swore, for she uttered her speech with an emphasis.

After dinner I went on board the ferry boat, and with a pretty good breeze, crossed the Narrows in half an hour to Long Island.

LONG ISLAND

At the entry of this bay is a little craggy island, about one or two miles long, called Coney Island. Before I came to New York Ferry I rid a byway, where in seven miles' riding I had twenty–four gates to open.

Dromo, being about twenty paces before me, stopped at a house, where, when I came up, I found him discoursing a negro girl, who spoke Dutch to him. "Dis de way to York?" says Dromo. "Yaw, dat is Yarikee," said the wench, pointing to the steeples. "What devil you say?" replies Dromo. "Yaw, mynheer," said the wench. "Damme you, what you say" said Dromo again. "Yaw, yaw," said the girl. "You a damn black bitch," said Dromo, and so rid on.

The road here for several miles is planted thick upon each side with rows of cherry–trees, like hedges, and the lots of land are mostly enclosed with stone fences.

YORK FERRY

At five in the afternoon I called at one Baker's that keeps the York Ferry, where, while I sat waiting for a passage, there came in a man and his wife that were to go over. The woman was a beauty, having a fine complexion and good features, black eyes and hair, and an elegant shape. She had an amorous look, and her eyes, methought, spoke a language which is universally understood. While she sat there her tongue never lay still, and tho' her discourse was of no great importance, yet methought her voice had music in it, and I was fool enough to be highly pleased to see her smiles at every little impertinence she uttered. She talked of a neighbour of hers that was very ill, and said she was sure she would die, for last night she had dreamt of nothing but white horses and washing of linen. I heard this stuff with as much pleasure as if Demosthenes or Cicero had been exerting their best talents, but meantime was not so stupid but I knew that it was the fine face and eyes, and not the discourse that charmed me. At six o'clock in the evening I landed at New York.

This city makes a very fine appearance for above a mile all along the river, and here lies a great deal of shipping. I put my horses up at one Waghorn's at the sign of the Cart and Horse. There I fell in with a company of toapers. Among the rest was an old Scotsman, by name Jameson, sheriff of the city, and two aldermen, whose names I know not. The Scotsman seemed to be dictator to the company; his talent lay in history, having a particular knack at telling a story. In his narratives he interspersed a particular kind of low wit, well known to vulgar understandings, and having a homely carbuncle kind of a countenance, with a hideous knob of a nose, he screwed it into a hundred different forms while he spoke, and gave such a strong emphasis to his words that he merely spit in one's face at three or four feet distance, his mouth being plentifully bedewed with salival juice by the force of the liquor which he drank and the fumes of the tobacco which he smoaked. The company seemed to admire him much, but he set me a–staring.

After I had sat some time with this polite company, Dr. Colchoun, surgeon to the fort, called in, to whom I delivered letters, and he carried me to the tavern,' which is kept by one Todd, an old Scotsman, to sup with the Hungarian Club, of which he is a member, and which meets there every night. The company were all strangers to me, except Mr. Home, Secretary of New Jersey, of whom I had some knowledge, he having been at my house at Annapolis. They saluted me very civilly, and I, as civilly as I could, returned their compliments, in neat short speeches, such as "Your very humble servant," "I 'm glad to see you," and the like commonplace phrases, used upon such occasions.We went to supper, and our landlord Todd entertained us, as he stood waiting, with quaint saws, and jackpudding speeches. "Praised be God," said he, "as to cuikry I defaa ony French cuik to ding me, bot a haggis is a dish I wadna tak the trouble to mak. Look ye, gentlemen, there was anes a Frenchman axed his frind to denner. His frind axed him, `What hae ye gotten till eat?' `Four an' twanty legs of mutton,' quo' he, `a' sae differently cuiked that ye winna ken whilk is whilk.' Sae whan he gaed there, what deel was it, think ye, but four and twanty sheep's trotters, be God"– he was a–going on with this tale of a tub when, very seasonably for the company, the bell, hastily pulled, called him to another room, and a little after we heard him roaring at the stair–head,–"Damn, ye bitch, wharfor winna ye bring a canle?"

After supper they set in for drinking, to which I was averse, and therefore sat upon nettles. They filled up bumpers at each round, but I would drink only three, which were to the King,' Governour Clinton,' and Governour Bladen,' which last was my own. Two or three toapers in the company seemed to be of opinion that a man could not have a more sociable quality or enduement than to be able to pour down seas of liquor, and remain unconquered, while others sank under the table. I heard this philosophical maxim, but silently dissented to it.

I left the company at ten at night pretty well flushed with my three bumpers, and ruminating on my folly went to my lodging at Mrs. Hogg's in Broad Street.

Saturday, June 16th.–I breakfasted with my landlady's sister, Mrs. Boswall. In the morning Dr. Colchoun called to see me, and he and I made an appointment to dine at Todd's. In the afternoon I took a turn thro' several of the principal streets in town, guarding against staring about me as much as possible, for fear of being remarked for a stranger, gaping and staring being the true criterion or proof of rustic strangers in all places. The following observations occurred to me:

I found the city less in extent, but by the stir and frequency upon the streets, more populous than Philadelphia. I saw more shipping in the harbour. The houses are more compact and regular, and in general higher built, most of them after the Dutch model, with their gavell ends fronting the street. There are a few built of stone; more of wood, but the greatest number of brick, and a great many covered with pantile and glazed tile with the year of God when built figured out with plates of iron, upon the fronts of several of them. The streets in general are but narrow, and not regularly disposed. The best of them run parallel to the river, for the city is built all along the water, in general.

This city has more of an urban appearance than Philadelphia. Their wharfs are mostly built with logs of wood piled upon a stone foundation. In the city are several large public buildings.

There is a spacious church,' belonging to the English congregation, with a pretty high, but heavy, clumsy steeple, built of freestone, fronting the street called Broadway. There are two Dutch churches, several other meetings, and a pretty large Town–house at the head of Broad street. The Exchange stands near the water, and is a wooden structure going to decay. From it a pier runs into the water called the Long Bridge, about fifty paces long, covered with plank and supported with large wooden posts. The Jews have one synagogue in this city.

The women of fashion here appear more in public than in Philadelphia, and dress much gayer. They come abroad generally in the cool of the evening and go to the Promenade.

I returned to my lodging at four o'clock, being pretty much tired with my walk. I found with Mrs. Boswall a handsome young Dutchwoman. We drank tea, and had a deal of trifling chat; but the presence of a pretty lady, as I hinted before, makes even trifling agreeable.

In the evening I writ letters to go by the post to Annapolis, and at night went and supped with the Hungarian Club at Todd's, where, after the bumpers began to go round according to their laudable custom, we fell upon various conversation, in which Todd, standing by, mixed a deal of his clumsy wit, which for the mere stupidity of it sometimes drew a laugh from the company. Our conversation ended this night with a piece of criticism upon a poem in the newspaper, where one of the company, Mr. M –e,' a lawyer, showed more learning than judgment in a disquisition he made upon nominatives and verbs, and the necessity there was for a verb to each nominative, in order to make sense. We dismissed at eleven o'clock.

Sunday, June 17th.–At breakfast I found with Mrs. Boswall some gentlemen, among whom was Mr. J ys,' an officer of the customs in New York. To me he seemed a man of an agreeable conversation and spirit. He had been in Maryland some years ago, and gave me an account of some of his adventures with the planters there. He showed me a deal of civility and complaisance, carried me to church, and provided me with a pew. The minister who preached to us was a stranger. He gave us a good discourse upon the Christian virtues. There was a large congregation of above a thousand, among whom was a number of dressed ladies. This church is above ioo feet long, and 8o wide. At the east end of it is a large semicircular area in which stands the altar, pretty well ornamented with painting and gilding.

The galleries are supported with wooden pillars of the Ionic order, with carved work of foliage and cherubs' heads gilt betwixt the capitals. There is a pretty organ at the west end of the church, consisting of a great number of pipes handsomely gilt and adorned; but I had not the satisfaction of hearing it play, they having at this time no organist; but the vocal music of the congregation was very good.

Mr J–ys carried me to Mr. Bayard's to dine, and at four o'clock we went to the coffee–house. I drank tea at a gentlewoman's house, whose name I know not, being introduced there by Mr. J–ys. There was an old lady and two young ones, her daughters, I suppose. The old lady's discourse ran upon news and politicks, but the young women sat mute, only now and then smiled at what was said, and Mr. Jeffrys enlivened the conversation with repartee.

At six o'clock I went to see the fort and battery. The castle, or fort, is now in ruins, having been burnt down three or four years ago by the conspirators, but they talk of repairing it again. The Lieutenant–Governour had here a house and a chapel, and there are fine gardens and terrace walks, from which one has a very pretty view of the city. In the fort are several guns, some of them brass and cast in a handsome mould. The new battery is raised with ramparts of turf, and the guns upon it are in size from twelve to eighteen pounders. The main battery is a great half–moon or semicircular rampart bluff upon the water, being turf upon a stone foundation, about ioo paces in length, the platform of which is laid in some places with plank, in others with flagstone. Upon it there are fifty–six great iron guns, well mounted, most of them being thirty–two pounders.

Mr. J–ys told me that to walk out after dusk upon this platform was a good way for a stranger to fit himself with a courtesan; for that place was the general rendezvous of the fair sex of that profession after sunset. He told me there was a good choice of pretty lasses among them, both Dutch and English. However, I was not so abandoned as to go among them, but went and supped with the Club at Todd's.

It appeared that our landlord was drunk, both by his words and actions. When we called for anything he hastily pulled the bell–rope, and when the servants came up, Todd had by that time forgot what was called for. Then he gave us a discourse upon law and gospel, and swore by God that he would prove that law was founded upon gospel, and gospel upon law, and that reason was depending upon both, and therefore to be a good lawyer it was substituted to be a good gospeller. We asked him what such a wicked dog as he had to do with gospel. He swore by God that he had a soul to be saved as well as the King, and he would neither be hanged nor damned for all the Kings in Christendom. We could not get rid of him till we put him in a passion by affirming he had no soul, and offering to lay him a dozen of wine that he could not prove he had one, at which, after some tags of incoherent arguments he departed the room in wrath, calling us heathens and infidels. I went home after twelve o'clock.

Monday, June 18th.–Most of this day proved rainy, and therefore I could not stir much abroad. I dined at Todd's with Dr. Colchounl and a young gentleman, a stranger. After dinner the doctor and I went to the coffee–house and took a hit at backgammon. He beat me two games. At five in the afternoon, I drank tea with Mrs. Boswall, and went to the coffee–house again, where I looked on while they played at chess. It continued to rain very hard. This night I shunned company, and went to bed at nine.

Tuesday, June 19th.–At breakfast with my landlady I found two strange gentlemen that had come from Jamaica. They had just such cloudy countenances as are commonly wore the morning alter a debauch in drinking. Our conversation was a medley, but the chief subject we went upon was the difference of climate in the American Provinces, with relation to the influence they had upon human bodies. I gave them as just an account as I could of Maryland, the air and temperature of that Province, and the distempers incident to the people there. I could not help suspecting that there were some physicians in the company by the tenour of the discourse, but could not understand for certain that any one there besides myself was a professed physician.

One gentleman there that came from Curaçao told us that in a month's time he had known either thirty or forty souls buried, which, in his opinion, was a great number for the small neighbourhood where he lived. I could scarce help laughing out at this speech, and was just going to tell him that I did not think it was customary to bury souls anywhere but in Ireland; but I restrained my tongue, having no mind to pick a quarrel for the sake of a joke.

We dined at Todd's, with seven in company, upon veal, beefsteaks, green pease, and raspberries for a dessert. There talking of a certain free negro in Jamaica, who was a man of estate, good sense, and education, the fore–mentioned gentleman who had entertained us in the morning about burying of souls, gravely asked if that negro's parents were not whites, for he was sure that nothing good could come of the whole generation of blacks.

Afternoon I drank tea with Mrs. Boswall, having, to pass away time, read some of the journal of proceedings against the conspirators' at New York. At night I went to a tavern fronting the Albany coffee–house along with Doctor Colchoun, where I heard a tolerable *concerto* of musick, performed by one violin and two German flutes. The violin was by far the best I had heard played since I came to America. It was handled by one Mr. H–d.

Wednesday, June 20th.–I dined this day at Todd's, where I met with one Mr. M –1s,' a minister at Shrewsbury in the jerseys, who had formerly been for some years minister at Albany. I made an agreement to go to Albany with him the first opportunity that offered. I inquired accordingly at the coffeehouse for the Albany sloops, but I found none ready to go.

I got acquainted with one Mr. Weemse, a merchant of Jamaica, my countryman and fellow lodger at Mrs. Hogg's.

He had come here for his health, being afflicted with the rheumatism. He had much of the gentleman in him, was good–natured, but fickle; for he determined to go to Albany and Boston in company with me; but, sleeping upon it, changed his mind. He drank too hard, whence I imagined his rheumatism proceeded more than from the intemperature of the Jamaica air.

After dinner I played backgammon with Mr. Jeffreys, in which he beat me two games for one. I read out the Journal of Proceedings, and–at night repared my baggage to go for Albany.

Thursday, June 21st.–I dined at Todd's with several gentlemen, and called upon Mr. M –Is at two o'clock, with whom I intended to go by water to Albany in a sloop belonging to one Knockson. I met here with one Mr. Knox, a young man, son of David Knox, late of Edinburgh, surgeon, in whose shop I had learnt pharmacy. While we talked over old stories, there passed some comic discourse betwixt Todd and four clumsy Dutchmen. These fellows asked him if they could all drink for fourpence. "That you may," says Todd, "such liquor as fourpence will afford."

So he brought them a bottle of ship–beer, and distributed it to them in a half–pint tumbler, the last of which being mostly froth, the Dutchman to whose share it came, looking angrily at Todd, said, "The Deyvil damn the carle!" "Damn the fallow," says Todd, "what wad he hae for his 4 pennies?" After getting my baggage and some provisions ready, I went on board the Albany sloop, where I found Mr. M –s and his wife, an old, jolly, fat Dutchwoman, mother to the Patroon at Albany, a gentleman there of Dutch extract, the chief landed man in the place.

NUTTING ISLAND

Having a contrary wind and an ebb tide, we dropped anchor about half a mile below New York, and went ashore upon Nutting Island, which is about half a mile in dimension every way, containing about sixty or seventy square acres. We there took in a cask of spring water.

One half of this island was made into hay, and upon the other half stood a crop of good barley, much damaged by a worm which they have here, which so soon as their barley begins to ripen cuts off the heads of it.

There lived an old Scots–Irishman upon this island with his family in a ruinous house, a tenant of the Governour's, to whom the island belongs *durante officio*. This old man treated us with a mug of ship–beer, and entertained us with a history of some of the adventures of the late Governour Cosby 1 upon that island. It is called Nutting Island from its bearing nuts in plenty, but what kind of nuts they are I know not, for I saw none there. I saw myrtle berries growing plentifully upon it, a good deal of juniper and some few plants of the ipecacuan. The banks of the island are stony and steep in some places. It is a good place to erect a battery upon, to prevent an enemy's approach to the town, but there is no such thing, and I believe that an enemy might land on the back of this island out of reach of the town battery and plant cannon against the city or even throw bombs from behind the island upon it.

We had on board this night six passengers, among whom were three women. They all could talk Dutch but myself and Dromo, and all but Mr. M–s seemed to prefer it to English. At eight o'clock at night, the tide serving us, we weighed anchor, and turned it up to near the mouth of North River, and dropt anchor again at ten just opposite to the great church in New York.

Friday, Tune 22d.–While we waited the tide in the morning, Mr. M–s and I went ashore to the house of one Mr. Van Dames, where we breakfasted, and went from thence to see the new Dutch church, a pretty large but heavy stone building, as most of the Dutch edifices are, quite destitute of taste or elegance. The pulpit of this church is prettily wrought, being of black walnut. There is a brass supporter for the great Bible that turns upon a swivel, and the pews are in a very regular order. The church within is kept very clean, and when one speaks or hollows there is a fine echo. We went up into the steeple, where there is one pretty large and handsome bell, cast at Amsterdam, and a publick clock. From this steeple we could have a full view of the city of New York.

Early this morning two passengers came on board of the sloop, a man and a woman, both Dutch. The man was named Marcus Van Bummill. He came on board drunk and gave us a surfeit of bad English. If anybody laughed when he spoke he was angry, being jealous that they thought him a fool. He had a good deal of the bully and braggadocio in him, but when thwarted or threatened he seemed faint–hearted and cowardly. Understanding that I was a valetudinarian he began to advise me how to manage my constitution. "You drink and whore too much," said he, "and that makes you thin and sickly. Could you abstain as I have done, and drink nothing but water for six weeks, and have to do with no women but your own lawful wife, your belly and cheeks would be like mine,–look ye, plump and smooth and round." With that he clapped his hands upon his belly and blowed up his cheeks like a trumpeter. He brought on board with him a runlet of rum, and, taking it into his head that somebody had robbed him of a part of it, he went down into the hold, and fell a–swearing bitterly by *Dunder, Sacramentum*, and *Jesu Christus*. I, being upon deck and hearing a strange noise below, looked down and saw him expanding his hands and turning up his eyes as if he had been at prayers. He was for having us all before a magistrate about it, but at last Knockson, the master of the sloop, swore him into good humour again, and persuaded him that his rum was all safe. He quoted a deal of scripture, but his favorite topics when upon that subject was about King David and King Solomon and the shape and size of the Tower of Babel. He pretended to have been mighty familiar with great folks when they came in his way, and this familiarity of his was so great as even to scorn and contemn them to their faces. After a deal of talk and rattle he went down and slept for four hours, and when he waked, imagined he had slept a whole day and a night, swearing it was Saturday night when it was only Friday afternoon. There was a Dutchwoman on board, remarkably ugly, upon whom this Van Bummill cast a loving eye, and wanted much to be at close conference with her.

GREENWITCH

At twelve o'clock we passed a little town, starboard, called Greenwitch, consisting of eight or ten neat houses, and two or three miles above that on the same shoar, a pretty box of a house, with an avenue fronting the river, belonging to Oliver Dulancie. On the left hand some miles above York, the land is pretty high and rocky, the west bank of the river for several miles being a steep precipice, above 100 feet high.

Mr. M–s read a treatise upon microscopes, and wanted me to sit and hear him, which I did, tho' with little relish, the piece being trite and vulgar, and tiresome to one who had seen Leewenhoek, and some of the best hands upon that subject. I soon found M–ls's ignorance of the thing, for as he read he seemed to be in a kind of surprise at every little trite observation of the author's. I found him an entire stranger to the mathematics, so as that he knew not the difference betwixt a cone and a pyramid, a cylinder and a prism. He had studied a year at Leyden under Boerhaave, even after he had entered into holy orders. He had once wore a soldier's livery, was very whimsical about affairs relating to farming, in so much that he had spent a deal of money in projects that way, but reaped as little profit as projectors commonly do. I was told by a gentleman that knew him that formerly he had been an immoderate drinker, so as to expose himself by it, but now he was so much reformed as to drink no liquor but water. In some parts of learning, such as the languages, he seemed pretty well versed. He could talk Latin and French very well, and read the Greek authors, and I was told that he spoke the Dutch to perfection. He inquired of me concerning Parson C–se of Maryland, but I could not find out which of the C ses it was. He told me he had once given him a hearty horsewhipping for some rude language lie gave him in a theological dispute which they had. I was informed by him that Morgan, the philosopher and mathematician, whom I had seen at Kingstown was his curate.

We passed a little country house belonging to one Philips at four o'clock, starboard. This house is about twenty miles above York. We had several learned discourses in the evening from Van Bummill concerning doctors. "You are a doctor," says he to me; "what signifies your knowledge? You pretend to know inward distempers and to cure them, but to no purpose; your art is vain. Find me out a doctor among the best of you, that can mend a man's body half so well as a joiner can help a crazy table or stool. I myself have spent more money on doctors than I would give for the whole tribe of them if I had it in my pocket again.

Experience has taught me to shun them as one would impostors and cheats, and now no doctor for me but the great Doctor above." This was the substance of his discourse, tho' it was not so well connected as I have delivered it. After this harangue he took a dram or two, and got again into his wonted raving humour. He took it in his head that Lord Baltimore was confined in the tower of Troy, as he called it, went down into the hold, and after he had there disgorged what was upon his stomach, he went to sleep and dreamt about it. He came upon deck a little before sunset, and was so full of it that he hailed each vessel that passed us, and told it as a piece of news.

We had a fresh westerly wind at night, which died away at ten o'clock, and we dropt anchor about forty miles above York.

Saturday, Tune 23d.–We weighed anchor about four in the morning, having the wind northeast and contrary, and the tide beginning to fall. We dropped anchor again at seven. Mr. Van Bummill was early upon deck, and was very inquisitive with Mr. M–s about the meaning of the word *superstition*, saying he had often met with that word in English books, but never could understand what was meant by it. Then he read us the 26th chapter of the Ecclesiasticus, concerning women, and after he had murdered the reading in the English, he read it from the Dutch Bible, and lectured upon it at large to the passengers and crew, and tho' he looked himself as grave as a parson, yet the company broke frequently out into fits of laughter.

We went ashore to fill water near a small log cottage on the west side of the river inhabited by one Stanespring and his family. The man was about thirty–seven years of age, and the woman thirty. They had seven children, girls and boys. The children seemed quite wild and rustic. They stared like sheep upon M–s and me when we entered the house, being amazed at my laced hat and sword. They went out to gather blackberries for us, which was the greatest present they could make us. In return for which we distributed among them a handful of copper halfpence. This cottage was very clean and neat, but poorly furnished, yet Mr. M–s observed several superfluous things which showed an inclination to finery in these poor people; such as a looking–glass with a painted frame, half a dozen pewter spoons, and as many plates, old and wore out, but bright and clean, a set of stone tea dishes and a teapot. These Mr. M ls said were superfluous, and too splendid for such a cottage, and therefore they ought to be sold to buy wool to make yarn; that a little water in a wooden pail might serve for a looking–glass, and wooden plates and spoons would be as good for use, and when clean would be almost as ornamental. As for the tea equipage it was quite unnecessary, but the man's musket, he observed, was as useful a piece of furniture as any in the cottage.

We had a pail of milk here, which we brought on board, and the wind coming southerly at eleven o'clock, we weighed anchor, and entered the Highlands, which presented a wild, romantic scene of rocks and mountains, covered with small scraggy wood, mostly oak.

ANTHONY'S NOSE–COOK'S ISLAND

WE passed Dunder Barrack, or Thunder Hill, larboard, at half an hour after eleven, and another hill, starboard, called Anthony's Nose from its resemblance to a man's nose, under which lies Cook's Island,' being a small rock about ten paces long and five broad, upon which is buried a certain cook of a man–of–war, from whom it got its name. His sepulchre is surrounded with ten or twelve small pine trees about twenty feet high, which make a grove over him. This wild and solitary place, where nothing presents but huge precipices and inaccessible steeps, where foot of man never was, infused in my mind a kind of melancholy, and filled my imagination with odd thoughts, which at the same time had something pleasant in them.

It was pretty to see the springs of water run down the rocks, and what entertained me not a little was to observe some pretty large oaks growing there, and their roots to appearance fixed in nothing but the solid stone, where you see not the least grain of mould or earth. The river is so deep in these Narrows of the Highlands that a large sloop may sail close upon the shore. We kept so near that the extremity of our boom frequently rustled among the leaves of the hanging branches from the bank. In some places of the channel here, there are ninety fathoms water, and very near the shore in several places seventy or sixty fathoms.

HAY RUCK

We passed the Hay Ruck,' a hill so called from its resemblance, upon our starboard at dinner time. There are several cottages here so very small that a man can scarce stand upright in them, and you would think that a strong fellow would carry his wooden but upon his back.

DOEPPER'S ISLAND

ABOUT three in the afternoon we cleared the Highlands, and left a small island called Doepper's or Dipper's Island' to the starboard. It is so named because, they say, it has been customary to dip strangers here, unless they make the sloop's crew drink, and by that they save their dipping and are made free in the river. Wherefore, as I never had been that way before, I saved my dipping with a bottle of wine which I spared them from my stores.

BUTTER MOUNTAIN–MURDER CREE

AT four o'clock we passed the Butter Mountain' on our larboard, above which is Murder Creek,' so called from a massacre of the white men that was committed by the Indians at the first settlement of the part.

DANCING HALL

AT six o'clock we passed Dancing Hall, larboard, a little square and level promontory, which runs about fifty paces into the river, overgrown with bushes, where they report, about sixty or seventy years ago, some young people from Albany, making merry and dancing, were killed by some Indians, who lay in ambush in the woods. We had a discourse this evening from Van Bummill about the Tower of Babel, which was his constant and darling theme. He told us that, in all his reading, he never could be informed of the height of it, and, as to its figure, he was pretty certain of that from the pictures of it which he had seen. When he had finished his argument, he got to talking a medley of Dutch and English to the women, which confusion of language was apropos after he had been busy about the Tower of Babel. The learned Van Bummill and the two Dutch women left us at seven o'clock, going ashore to a place two miles below Poughcapsy, I where they lived.

POUGHCAPSY

WE anchored at eight o'clock at the entry of that part of the river called Long Reach,' the weather being very thick and rainy, and close by us on the starboard side stood a small village called Poughcapsy, where the master and hands went ashore and left us to keep the sloop.

Sunday, Tune 24th.–At four in the morning Mr. M–s and I went ashore to the tavern, and there we met with a justice of the peace and a New–light tailor. The justice seemed to have the greatest half or all the learning of the county in his face, but so soon as he spoke, we found that he was no more learned than other men. The tailor's phiz was screwed up to a satisfied pitch, and he seemed to be either under great sorrow for his sins or else a–hatching some mischief in his heart, for I have heard that your hypocritical rogues always put on their most solemn countenance or vizard, when they are contriving how to perpetrate their villanies. We soon discovered that this tailor was a Moravian.

The Moravians are a wild, fanatick sect with which both this place and the jerseys are pestered. They live in common, men and women mixed in a great house or barn, where they sometimes eat and drink, sometimes sleep, and sometimes preach and howl, but are quite idle, and will employ themselves in no useful work. They think all things should be in common, and say that religion is entirely corrupted by being too much blended with the laws of the country. They call their religion the true religion, or the religion of the Lamb, and they commonly term themselves the followers of the Lamb, which I believe is true, in so far as some of them may be wolves in sheep's clothing. This sect was first founded by a German enthusiast, Count Zenzindorff, who used to go about some years ago and persuade the people to his opinions and drop a certain catechism, which he had published, upon the highway. They received a considerable strength and addition to their numbers by Whitefield's preaching in these parts, but now are upon the decline, since there is no opposition made to them.

Mr. M–ls and I anatomized this Moravian tailor in his own hearing, and yet he did not know of it, for we spoke Latin. He asked what language that was. The justice told him he believed it was Latin, at which the cabbager sighed and said it was a pagan language. We treated him, however, with a dram, and went from the tavern to one Cardevitz's, who having the rheumatism in his arm, asked my advice, which I gave him. The land here is high and woody. and the air very cool.

SOPUS VILLAGE

We weighed anchor at seven o'clock, with the wind southwest and fresh, and half an hour after passed by Sopus, a pleasant village situated upon the west side of the river, famous for beer and ale.

LITTLE SOPUS ISLAND

Little above that is a small island called Little Sopus, which is about half way betwixt Albany and irk. At Sopus we passed by the Governour's fleet, consisting of three painted sloops. That therein Clinton was had the union flag astern. He had been at Albany treating with the Indians.

BLUE MOUNTAINS

We now had a sight of the range of mountains called the Catskill or Blue Mountains, bearing pretty ar N. W. and capped with clouds. Here the river about two miles broad, and the land low, green, and pleasant. Large open fields, and thickets of woods, alternately mixed, entertain the eye with variety of landscips.

ANCRUM

AT twelve o'clock we sailed by Ancrum, starboard, the seat of Mr. Livingston, a lawyer, where he has a fine brick house standing close upon the river. The wind blew very high att south east. AT half an hour after twelve we saw the town of Ransbeck, a German town, starboard, in which are two churches.

LIVINGSTON MANOR

AT one o'clock we scudded by Livingston Manor, then the Catskill Hills bore west by south. At three o'clock we sailed by a Lutheran chapel, larboard, where we could see the congregation dismissing, divine service being over.

CARMINE ISLAND

AT four o'clock we passed by Carmine Island,' about three miles in length.

NUSSMAN'S ISLAND

At five we sailed past Nussman's Island,' starboard, where there is a small nation of the Mochacander Indians, with a king that governs them. We ran aground upon a sandbank at half an hour after five o'clock, and by hard labour got clear again in about an hour. This was a great disappointment to us, for we expected that night to reach Albany. There came up a thunder gust as soon as we got clear, which obliged us to furl our sails and fix our anchor; but it soon went over, so with a small wind we made three miles farther, and passed a sloop bound for York, where some fine folks were on board. At eight o'clock there came up a hard storm with very sharp thunder, so that we were obliged to let go our anchor again, and there remain all night.

Monday, June 25th.–We went ashore this morning upon a farm belonging to 'Cobus Ranslaer,l brother to the Patroon' at Albany. (*James* by the Dutch appellation is *'Cobus*, being *Jacobus* contracted.) There is here a fine saw mill that goes by water.

At seven o'clock, the wind being southerly, we hoised anchor, and, sailing up the river, we passed large stone, larboard, called Prec Stone, or Preaching Stone,' from its resemblance to a pulpit. We ad not made much way, before the wind changed northwest, so we resolved to go to Albany in the loop's canoe, and went ashore to borrow another carry our baggage. We found the poor people here in great terror of the Indians, they being apprehensive that they would begin their old trade of scalping.

ALBANY

WE set off in the canoes at nine o'clock, and saw Albany at a distance. We landed upon an island,' belonging to Mr. M–s, upon which there was fine grass of different sorts, and very good crops of wheat and pease, of which they bring up great quantities here for the use of the ships,–the bug not getting into their pease there as with us. These were the first fields of pease I had seen since I left Britain. We met several Dutchmen on the island, who had rented *morgans* of land upon it; they call half an acre of land there a *morgan*.

These people were very inquisitive about the news, and told us of a Frenchman and his wife that had been at Albany the day before we arrived. They had come from Canada, and it was they we saw on board the sloop that passed us last night. The Frenchman was a fugitive, according to his own account, and said he had been a priest, and was expelled from his convent for having an intrigue with that lady who was now his wife. The lady had been prosecuted at law and had lost the greatest part of her estate, which went amongst these cormorants, the lawyers. The Governour of Canada, Mons'r Bonharnois, being her enemy, she could not expect justice, and therefore fled with this priest to the English settlements, in order to prevent her being entirely beggared, taking the residue of her estate along with her.

This Bonharnois is now a very old man, and they say behaves himself tyrannically in this government. He was a courtier in Louis XIVth's time, and then went by the name of Mons'r Bon Vit, which being an ugly name in the French language, the King changed his name to Bonharnois.

This day there came some Canada Indians in two canoes to Albany to pursue this priest and his lady. 15,000 livres were laid upon each of their heads by the Governour. They said they had orders to bring back the priest, dead or alive; if dead to scalp him, and take the consecrated flesh from his thumb and forefinger. The lady they were to bring back alive; but they came too late to catch their game.

Mr. M–s imagined that all this story was a plausible fiction, and that the Frenchman was sent among them as a spy; but this conception of his to me seemed improbable.

Tuesday, June 26th.–Early this morning I went with Mr. M –s to Albany, being a pleasant walk of two miles from the island. We went a small mile out of town to the house of Jeremiah Ranslaer, who is dignified here with the title of Patroon. He is the principal landed man in these parts, having a large manor, forty–eight miles long and twenty–four broad, bestowed upon his greatgrandfather by King Charles the Second, after his restoration. The old man, it seems, had prophesied his recovering of his kingdoms ten years before it happened. The King had been his lodger when he was in Holland, and thereby he had an opportunity to ingratiate himself, and procure the royal favour. This manor is divided into two equal halves by Hudson's River, and the city of Albany stands in the middle of it. This city pays him a good yearly rent for the liberty of cutting their firewood.

The Patroon is a young man, of a good mien and presence. He is a bachelor, nor can his friends persuade him to marry. By paying too much homage to Bacchus, he has acquired a hypochondriac habit. He has a great number of tenants upon his manor, and he told me himself that he could muster 600 men fit to bear arms. Mr. M –s and I dined at his house, and were handsomely entertained with good viands and wine. After dinner he showed us his garden and parks, and Mr. M –s got into one of his long harangues of farming and improvement of ground.

At four o'clock M–s and I returned to town, where M–s having a general acquaintance (for he had practised physick ten years in the city, and was likewise the Church of England minister there), he introduced me into about twenty or thirty houses, where I went thro' the farce of kissing most of the women, a manner of salutation which is expected (as M–s told me) from strangers coming there. I told him it was very well, if he led the way I should follow, which he did with clerical gravity. This might almost pass for a penance, for the generality of the women here, both old and young, are remarkably ugly.

At night we went to the island, where we supped. While we were at supper we smelt something very strong like burnt oatmeal, which they told me was an animal called a skunk, the urine of which could be smelt at a great distance, something of the nature of the polecat, but not quite so disagreeable.

Wednesday, June 27th.–I went this morning with the Patroon's brother, Stephen Ranslaer, to see the Cohoos, a great fall of water twelve miles above Albany.

COHOOS

THE water falls over a rock almost perpendicular, eighty feet high and nine hundred feet broad, and the noise of it is easily heard at four miles' distance; but in the spring of the year, when the ice breaks, it is heard like great guns all the way at Albany. There is a fine mist scattered about where it falls, for above half a mile below it, upon which when the sun shines opposite appears a pretty rainbow. Near the fall the noise is so great that you cannot discern a man's voice, unless he hollows pretty loud. Below the fall the river is very narrow and very deep, running in a rocky channel. There is a bank of solid rock, about 300 or 400 feet wide, as smooth and level as a table.

In this journey we met a Mohook Indian and his family going a–hunting. His name was Solomon. He had a squaw with him, over whom he seemed to have an absolute authority.

We travelled for two miles thro' impenetrable woods, this Indian being our guide, and when we came to the banks of the river near the falls we were obliged to leave our horses and descend frightful precipices. One might walk across the river on foot upon the top of the rock whence the water falls, was it not for fear of being carried down by the force of the water, and Solomon told us that the Indians sometimes run.

MOHOOKS TOWN

We rid at a pretty hard rate fifteen or sixteen miles farther to the Mohooks town, standing upon the same river. In it there are several wooden and brick houses, built after the Dutch fashion, and some Indian wigwams or huts, with a church where one Barclay 2 preaches to a congregation of Indians in their own language, for the bulk of the Mohooks up this way are Christians.

Returning from here we dined at Col. Skuyler's,3 about four o'clock in the afternoon, who is naturalized amon_– the Indians, can speak several of their languages, and has lived for years among them. We spent part of the evening at the Patroon's, and going to town at night I went to the tavern with Mr. Livingston, a man of estate and interest there, where we had a mixed conversation.

SCHENECTADY

Thursday, June 28th.–Early this morning I took horse, and went in company with one Collins,' a surveyor here, to a village called Schenectady, about sixteen miles from Albany, and pleasantly situated upon the Mohook River.

It is a trading village, the people carrying on a traffick with the Indians; their chief commodities, wampum, knives, needles, and other such pedlery ware. This village is pretty near as large as Albany, and consists chiefly of brick houses, built upon a pleasant plain, enclosed all round at about a mile's distance, with thick pine woods. These woods form a copse above your head, almost all the way betwixt Albany and Schenectady, and you ride over a plain, level, sandy road till, coming out of the covert of the woods, all at once the village strikes surprisingly your eye, which I can compare to nothing but the curtain rising in a play and displaying a beautiful scene.

We returned to M–s's island, from whence between twelve and one o'clock I went to Albany in a canoe, the day being somewhat sultry, tho' in this latitude the heats are tolerable to what they are two or three degrees to the southward, the mornings and evenings all summer long being cool and pleasant, but often, about noon and for three hours after, the sun is very hot.

I went to see the school in this city, in which are about aoo scholars, boys and girls. I dined at the Patroon's; after dinner Mr. Shakesburrough, surgeon to the fort, came in, who by his conversation seemed to have as little of the quack in him as any half–hewn doctor ever I had met with. The doctors in Albany are mostly Dutch, all empirics, having no knowledge or learning but what they have acquired by bare experience. They study chiefly the virtues of herbs, and the woods there furnish their shops with all the pharmacy they use.

A great many of them take the care of a family for the value of a Dutch dollar a year, which makes the practice of physick a mean thing, and unworthy of the application of a gentleman. The doctors here are all barbers.

This afternoon I went a–visiting with M –s, and had the other kissing bout to go thro'. We went at night to Stephen Ranslaer's, where we supped.

Friday, June 29th.–After breakfast I walked out with M–s, and visited some more old women, where I had occasion to prescribe and enter into a dispute with a Dutch doctor. Mr. M s's gesture in, common discourse often afforded me subject of speculation. At every the least trifling expression and common sentence in discourse, he would shrug up his shoulders, and stare one in the face as if he had uttered some very wonderful thing, and he would do the same while another person spoke, tho' he expressed nothing but common chat. By this means it was hard to tell when anything struck his fancy, for by this odd habit he had contracted in his gesture, everything seemed alike to raise his admiration. About this time one Kuyler, the mayor of the city, was suspected of trading with the Canada Indians, and selling powder to them. The people in town spoke pretty openly of it, and the thing coming to Governour Clinton's ears, he made him give security for his appearance at the General Court, to have the affair tried and canvassed.

I went before dinner with M –s, and saw the inside of the Town–house.' The great hall where the court sits is about forty feet long and thirty broad. This is a clumsy, heavy building, both without and within. We went next and viewed the workmen putting up new palisading or stoccadoes to fortify the town, and at ten o'clock we walked to the island, and returned to town again at twelve. Mr. M –s and I dined upon cold gammon at one Stevenson's, a Scots gentleman of some credit there. We drank tea at Steph. Ranslaer's, and supped at widow Skuyler's, where the conversation turned upon the Moravian enthusiasts and their doctrines.

Saturday, June 30th.–In the morning I went with M –s to make some more visits, of which I was now almost tired. Among others we went to see Dr. Rosaboom,2 one of the Dutch medicasters of the place, a man of considerable practice in administering physick and shaving. He had a very voluminous Dutch Herbalist lying on the table before him, being almost a load for a London porter. The sight of this made me sick, especially when I understood it was writ in High Dutch. I imagined the contents of it were very weighty and ponderous, as well as the book itself. It was writ by one *Rumpertus Dodonzus.* From this book Rosaboom had extracted all his learning in physick, and he could quote no other author but the great infallible Rumpertus, as he styled him. His discourse to us tended very much to self–commendation, being an historical account of cases in surgery, where he had had surprising success.

At ten o'clock M–s and I went to the island, where we dined, and M –s, being hot with walking, went to drink his cool water as usual, which brought an ague upon him, and he was obliged to go to bed. In the meantime the old woman and I conversed for half an hour about a rural life and good husbandry. At three o'clock I walked abroad to view the island, and sitting under a willow near the water, I was invited to sleep, but scarce had I enjoyed half an hour's repose, when I was waked by a cow that was eating up my handkerchief, which.

I had put under my head. I pursued her for some time before I recovered it, when I suppose the snuff in it made her disgorge, but it was prettily pinked all over with holes.

I went to the house and drank tea and then walked to town with M–s. On the way we met an old man who goes by the name of Scots Willie. He had been a soldier in the garrison, but was now discharged as an invalid. He told us he had been at the battle of Killiecrankie in Scotland, upon the side where Lord Dundee fought, and that he saw him fall in the battle.

We supped by invitation at the tavern with some of the chief men in the city, it being muster day, and a treat given by the officers of the fort to the muster masters. There were Messrs. Kuyler the Mayor, Tansbrook the Recorder, Holland the Sheriff,' Surveyor Collins,' Captain Blood, Captain Haylin c of the Fort, and several others. The conversation was rude and clamorous, but the viands and wine were good. We had news of the French having taken another small fort, besides Cansoe. I walked with M–s to ye island at ten at night.

Sunday, July 1st.–At six o'clock this morning a sharp thunder gust came up with a heavy rain. I breakfasted at the island, and went to town with M–s and his wife. At ten o'clock we went to the English Church,' where was the meanest congregation ever I beheld, there not being above fifteen or twenty in church, besides the soldiers of the fort, who sat in a gallery. M–s preached and gave us an indifferent good discourse against worldly riches, the text being, "It is easier for a cable [camel] to pass thro' the eye of a needle than for a rich man to enter the kingdom of heaven." This discourse, he told me, was calculated for the natural vice of that people, which was avarice, and particularly for Mr. Livingston,' a rich but very covetous man in. town, who valued himself much for his riches. But unfortunately Livingston did not come to church to hear his reproof.

At twelve o'clock another thunder gust came up. We dined at Stephen Ranslaer's, and made several visits in the afternoon. Among the rest we went to see Captain Blood, of the fort. He is nephew to the famous Blood' that stole the Crown. This man is a downright old soldier, having in his manner an agreeable mixture of roughness and civility. He expressed a strong regard for the memory of the Duke of Berwick, of whose death, when he heard, he could not forbear crying, for tho' he was an enemy to his master, the King of England, yet was he a brave and a generous man, for when he and several other English officers were taken prisoners in battle by the French, the duke generously gave them liberty upon their parole, and lent or indeed gave them ter pistoles apiece to furnish their pockets when they were quite bare of money. This spirit of gratitude in the old man pleased me very much, and made me conceive a good opinion of him, gratitude being a certain criterion or mark of a generous mind.

After visiting him we went to Captain Haylin's house, who received us very civilly, but not in such a polite manner as Captain Blood. He told us he had been a dragoon at the siege of Namur in King William's time and was then twenty years old, which makes him an older man than Blood, whose first campaign was the battle of Almanza.

I observed the streets of this city to be most crowded upon Sunday evening, especially with women. We supped at Stephen Ranslaer's.

Monday, July 2d.– I now began to be quite tired of this place, where there was no variety or choice, either of company or conversation, and one's ears perpetually invaded and molested with volleys of rough–sounding Dutch, which is the language most in use here. I therefore spoke to one Wendall, master of a sloop, which was to sail this evening for York, and took my passage in him. I laid in a stock of provisions for the voyage at one Miller's, a sergeant of the fort, who keeps the tavern, and where my landlady, happening to be a Scotswoman, was very civil and obliging to me for country's sake. She made me a present of a dried tongue. As I talked with her a certain ragged fellow came bluntly up, and took me by the hand, naming me. "Sir," says he, "there is a gentleman here in town who says he knows you, and has been in your garden at Annapolis in Maryland, when he lived with one Mr. Dulany there. He swears by G–d he would be glad to see you to talk a little or so, as it were, about friends and acquaintances there.

He bid me tell you so, and damme, says I, if I don't, so I hope the gentleman won't be offended." I told him no, there was no offence, but bid him give my service to my friend, and tell him I was now in a hurry, and could not wait upon him, but some other time would do as well. So, giving this orator a dram, I went and drank half a pint with the Captains Blood and Haylin, and walked to the island, where I dined.

In the afternoon I read Rollin's *Belles Lettres*. The day was hazy and threatened rain very much. At half an hour after two o'clock I saw Wendall's sloop falling down the river, with the tide, and they having given me the signal of a gun, which was agreed upon, they sent their canoe for me. At three o'clock I took my leave of M –s and his wife, thanking them for all their civilities and the hospitality I had met with in their house. I followed the sloop for near two miles in the canoe, before I overtook her, and went on board half an hour after three.

We had scarce been half an hour under sail after I came on board when we ran aground upon some shoals about a mile above the oversleigh and dropt anchor, till after six, the tide rising, we were afloat again, and went down, with the wind N. by East.,–rainy.

There was a negro fellow on board, who told me he was a piece of a fiddler, and played some scraping tunes to one Wilson, who had come on board of us in a canoe. This was an impudent fellow. He accosted me with "How do you, countryman?" at first sight, and told me he was a Scotsman, but I soon found by his howl in singing the *Black Jock* to the negro fiddle that he was a genuine Teague. He told me some clever lies, and claimed kin to Arncaple in Scotland. He said he had an estate of houses by heritage in Glasgow, swore he was born a gentleman for five generations, and never intended for the plough; therefore he had come to push his fortune in these parts.

At seven o'clock we reached the oversleigh, and there ran aground again. In the meantime a Dutch gentleman, one Volckert Douw, came on board a passenger, and I flattered myself I should not be quite alone, but enjoy some conversation; but I was mistaken, for the devil a word but Dutch was bandied about betwixt the sailors and him, and in general there was such a medley of Dutch and English as would have tired a horse. We heaved out our anchor, and got off the shoal at half an hour after seven, so got clear of the oversleigh, the only troublesome part in the whole voyage. We sailed four miles below it, the wind northeast and the night very rainy and dark. We dropt anchor at nine at night and went to bed.

The city of Albany lies on the west side of Hudson's River upon a rising hill about thirty or forty miles below where the river comes out of the lake, and 16o miles above New York.

The hill whereon it stands faces the southeast. The city consists of three pretty compact streets, two of which run parallel to the river, and are pretty broad, and the third cuts the other two at right angles, running up towards the fort, which is a square stone building, about Zoo feet square, with a bastion at each corner, each bastion mounting eight or ten great guns, most of them thirty–two pounders. In the fort are two large brick houses facing each other, where there is lodging for the soldiers.

There are three market houses in this city, and three public edifices, upon two of which are cupolas or spires, viz., upon the Townhouse and the Dutch church. The English church is a great, heavy stone building without any steeple, standing just below the fort.

The greatest length of the streets is half a mile.

In the fort is kept a garrison of 300 men under the King's pay, who now and then send reinforcements to Oswego, a frontier garrison and trading town, lying about i8o miles south and by west of Albany. This city is enclosed by a rampart or wall of wooden palisadoes, about ten feet high and a foot thick, being the trunks of pine–trees rammed into the ground, pinned close together, and ending each in a point at top. Here they call them stoccadoes. At each 200 feet distance, round this wall is a block house, and from the north gate of the city runs a thick stone wall down into the river, 200 feet long, at each end of which is a block house. In these block houses about fifty of the city militia keep guard every night, and the word all's well walks constantly round all night long from sentry to sentry and round the fort. There are five or six gates to this city, the chief of which are the north and the south gates. In the city are about 4,000 inhabitants, mostly Dutch or of Dutch extract.

The Dutch here keep their houses very neat and clean, both without and within. Their chamber floors are generally laid with rough plank, which in time, by constant rubbing and scrubbing, becomes as smooth as if it had been planed. Their chambers and rooms are large and handsome. They have their beds generally in alcoves, so that you may go thro' all the rooms of a great house and see never a bed. They affect pictures much, particularly scripture history, with which they adorn their rooms. They set out their cabinets and *buffets* much with china. Their kitchens are likewise very clean, and there they hang earthen or delft plates and dishes all round the walls, in manner of pictures, having a hole drilled thro' the edge of the plate or dish, and a loop of ribbon put into it to hang it by; but notwithstanding all this nicety and cleanliness in their houses they are in their persons slovenly and dirty. They live here very frugally and plain, for the chief merit among them seems to be riches, which they spare no pains or trouble to acquire, but are a civil and hospitable people in their way, but at best rustic and unpolished.

I imagined when I first came there that there were some very rich people in the place. They talked of thirty, forty, fifty, and a hundred thousand pounds as of nothing, but I soon found that their riches consisted more in large tracts of land than in cash.

They trade pretty much with the Indians, and have their manufactories for wampum, a good Indian commodity. It is of two sorts,–the black, which is the most valuable, and the white wampum. The first kind is a bead made out of the bluish black part of a clam shell.

It is valued at six shillings, York money, per one hundred beads. The white is made of a conch shell from the West Indies, and is not so valuable. They grind the beads to a shape upon a stone, and then with a well–tempered needle dipped in wax and tallow they drill a hole thro' each bead. This trade is apparently trifling, but would soon make an estate to a man that could have a monopoly of it, being in perpetual demand among the Indians, from their custom of burying quantities of it with their dead. They are very fond of it, and they will give skins or money or anything for it, having (tho' they first taught the art of making it to the Europeans) lost the art of making it themselves.

They live in their houses in Albany as if it were in prisons, all their doors and windows being perpetually shut. But the reason of this may be the little desire they have for conversation and society, their whole thoughts being turned upon profit and gain, which necessarily makes them live retired and frugal. At least this is the common character of the Dutch everywhere. But indeed the excessive cold winters here oblige them in that season to keep all snug and close, and they have not summer sufficient to revive heat in their veins, so as to make them uneasy or put it in their heads to air themselves. They are a healthy, long–lived people, many in this city being in age near or above 100 years, and eighty is a very common age. They are subject to rotten teeth and scorbutic gums, which, I suppose, is caused by the cold air, and their constant diet of salt provisions in the winter; for in that season they are obliged to lay in, as for a sea voyage, there being no stirring out of doors then for fear of never stirring again. As to religion they have little of it among them, and of enthusiasm not a grain. The bulk of them, if anything, are of the Lutheran Church.

Their women in general, both old and young, are the hardest favoured ever I beheld. Their old women wear a comical head–dress, large pendants, short petticoats, and they stare upon one like witches.

They generally eat to their morning's tea raw hung beef, sliced down in thin chips in the manner of parmesan cheese. Their winter here is excessive cold, so as to freeze their cattle stiff in one night in the stables.

To this city belong about twenty–four sloops about fifty tons burden, that go and come to York. They chiefly carry plank and rafters. The country about is very productive of hay and good grain, the woods not much cleared.

The neighbouring Indians are the Mohooks to the northwest, the Canada Indians to the northward, and to the southward a small scattered nation of the Mohackanders.

The young men here call their sweethearts *luffees*, and a young fellow of eighteen is reckoned a simpleton if he has not a *luffee*; but their women are so homely that a man must never have seen any other *luffees else they will never entrap him.*

Tuesday, July 3d.–We sailed for some time betwixt one and three in the morning, and then, the tide turning against us, we dropt anchor.

MUSSMAN'S ISLAND

We weighed at six in the morning and passed Nussman's Island, larboard,–wind north and by east. At half an hour after seven we met two sloops from York by whom we had news of a French privateer taken by Captain Ting, master of the Boston galley.

KENDERHUICK–VANSKRUIK

At nine o'clock we passed the Kenderhuick, a small peninsula called Vanskruik, where stood a farr house, and the fields were covered with good grai and hay. About this time two Dutchmen in a batteau came on board of us, and fastened the batteau to the sloop's side. The wind freshened up an was fair.

BLUE MOUNTAINS

WE could now observe the Catskill Mountains bearing southwest, starboard. At half an hour after ten, the wind freshened so much that the batteau broke loose from the sloop and overset, and one of the Dutchmen that was stepping down to save her was almost drowned. The fellows scampered away for blood in our canoe to recover their cargo and loading, which was all afloat upon the water, consisting of old jackets, breeches, bags, wallets, and buckets.

This kept us back some miles, for we were obliged to drop our anchor to stay for our canoe.

They picked up all their goods and chattels again, excepting a small hatchet which by its ponderosity went to the bottom, but the rest of the cargo, being old clothes, rope ends, and wooden tackle, floated on the surface.

My fellow passenger, Mr. Douw, was very devout all this morning. He kept poring upon Whitefield's sermons.

KEMP

At twelve o'clock we passed a place called the Kemp, larboard, where some High Germans are settled. The Catskill Mountains bore W. by S.

HYBANE AND MURLANIN ISLANDS

At one o'clock we passed Hybane and Murlanin Islands, larboard. The Catskill Mountains bore due west.

SOPUS CREEK–LITTLE SOPUS ISLAND

At three o'clock we cleared Sopus Creek, otherwise called Murder Creek, starboard, and half an hour after four, Little Sopus Island, reckoned half way betwixt Albany and York. Catskill Mountains bore west northwest.

POUGH CAPSY

At half an hour after seven we passed by Poughcapsy, larboard. We sailed all night but slowly, our wind failing us. 268.

Wednesday, July 4th.–At two in the morning, the wind dying away, and the tide being against us, we dropt anchor five miles to the northward of the Highlands. I got up by five in the morning, and going upon deck I found a scattered fog upon the water, the air cold and damp and a small wind at south. The ebb tide began at six in the morning, so we weighed anchor and tripped it down with a pretty strong southerly wind in our teeth.

DOEPPER'S ISLAND–HIGHLANDS

At ten o'clock we passed Doepper's Island, larboard, and as we entered the Highlands the wind left us. At half an hour after ten, the wind turned fair at northeast, but small; at twelve southerly again; at half an hour after two very variable, but settled at last in the southerly quarter.

COMMASKY, OR BUTTERMILK ISLAI

We came opposite to a little log–house, or cottage, upon the top of a high, steep precipice in view of Commasky, or Buttermilk Island, where we dropt anchor. The tide beginning to flow, we went ashore to this house in expectation of some milk or fowls or fresh provision, but could get none, for the people were extremely poor. This appeared a very wild, romantic place, surrounded with huge rocks, dreadful precipices, and scraggy, broken trees.

The man's name that inhabited here was James Williams, a little old man, that followed fishing and cutting of timber rafters to send to Albany or York. He had four children,– three sons and a daughter, whom he kept all employed about some work or other. I distributed a few copper halfpence among them, for which they gave me a great many country bows and curtsies. It is surprising how these people in the winter time live here or defend themselves in such slight houses against the violent cold.

Going on board again at 4 o'clock I killed a snake, which I had almost trod upon as I clambered down the steep. Had it been a rattlesnake I should have been entitled to a colonel's commission, for it is a common saying here that a man has no title to that dignity until he has killed a rattlesnake.

The rock here is so steep that you may stand within twenty yards of the edge of the bank, and yet not see the river, altho' it is very near a mile broad in this place. The tide ebbing at half an hour after six we weighed anchor, and found by the tiresome length of our cable that there were ninety feet water within twenty paces of the shoar.

HAY RUCK

We passed by the Hay Ruck, half an hour after seven, the wind southwest. We sent our canoe ashore here to a farmhouse, and got a bucketful of buttermilk and a pail of sweet milk.

ANTHONY's NOSE–COOK'S ISLAND

AT half an hour after eight we passed Anthony's Nose, larboard, wind strong at south; at nine Cook's Island, larboard; at ten cleared the Highlands, and anchored at two in the morning some miles below the Highlands.

Thursday, July 5th.–We weighed anchor a little after six in the morning, wind southwest, and dropt anchor again a quarter after two in the afternoon, York Island being in view at a distance. We went ashore to the house of one Kaen Buikhaut, a Dutch farmer. The old man was busy in making a sleigh, which is a travelling machine used here and at Albany in the winter time to run upon the snow. The woman told us she had eighteen children, nine boys and as many girls. Their third daughter was a handsome girl, about sixteen years of age. We purchased there three fat fowls for ninepence, and a great bucketful of milk into the bargain. We went on board a quarter after six, and had hard work in weighing, our anchor having got fast hold of a rock. Dromo grinned like a pagod as he tugged at the cable, or like one of his own country idols.

However, we got it up at length. At ten at night we had a very hard southerly wind and had almost lost our canoe. The wind came up so furious that we were obliged to drop anchor at eleven o'clock. Another sloop, running like fury before the wind, had almost been foul of us in the dark till we gave her the signal of a gun, which made her bear awav.

YORK ISLAND- GREENWITCH

Friday, July 6th.–We weighed anchor before five in the morning, having the ebb tide, the wind still southerly, and the weather rainy. We came up with York Island and Dulancie's house' at half an hour after six, larboard. Here we were becalmed, and so floated with the tide till nine o'clock, Greenwitch larboard. The wind sprang up at northwest very fresh with a heavy shower, and about half an hour after nine we landed at New York.

NEW YORK

I never was so destitute of conversation in my life as in this voyage. I heard nothing but Dutch spoke all the way. My fellow passenger Volkert Douw could speak some English, but had as little in him to enliven conversation as any young fellow ever I knew that looked like a gentleman. Whoever had the care of his education had foundered him by instilling into him enthusiastic religious notions.

At ten o'clock I went to my lodging at Mrs. Hogg's, where I first heard the melancholy news of the loss of the Philadelphia privateer. I dined at Todd's, where there was a mixed company; among the rest Mr. H–n, the City Recorder, Oliver Dulancie, and a gentleman in a green coat, with a scarified face, whose name I cannot recollect, from Antigua. After dinner they went to the old trade of bumpering; therefore I retired.

In this company there was one of these despicable fellows whom we may call c–t spies, a man, as I understood, pretty intimate with G–r C–n, who might perhaps share some favour for his dexterity in intelligence. This fellow I found made it his business to foist himself into all mixed companies to hear what was said and to inquire into the business and character of strangers. After dinner I happened to be in a room near the porch fronting the street, and overheard this worthy intelligencer a–pumping of Todd, the landlord. He was inquiring of him who that gentleman in the green coat was whom I just now mentioned. Todd replied "He is a gentleman from Antigua, who comes recommended to C–re W–n, by Governour G–h, of Virginia," and that he had been with Lord Banff, and left him upon some disgust or quarrel. Todd next informed him who I was, upon his asking the question. "You mean the pockfretten man," said he, "with the dark–coloured silk coat. He is a countryman of mine, by God,–one Hamilton from Maryland. They say he is a doctor, and is travelling for his health." Hearing this stuff, "this is afternoon news," thought I, "for the Governour," and just as the inquisitor was desiring Todd to speak lower (he was not deaf), I bolted out upon them and put an end to the inquiry, and the inquisitor went about his business.

I went to the inn to see my horses, and finding them in good plight, Mr. Waghorn desired me to walk into a room, where were some Boston gentlemen that would be company for me in my journey there. I agreed to set out with them for Boston upon Monday morning. Their names were Messrs. Laughton and Parker,' by employment traders. There was in company an old grave don, who, they told me, was both a parson and physician.

Being a graduate, he appeared to be in a mean attire. His wig was remarkably weather–beaten, the hairs being all as straight as a rush, and of an orange yellow at the extremities; but that it had been once a fair wig you might know by the appearance of that part which is covered by the hat, for that headwear I suppose seldom went off unless at proper times to yield place to his nightcap. The uncovered part of his wig had changed its hue by the sunbeams and rain alternately beating upon it. This old philosopher had, besides, as part of his wearing apparel, a pair of old greasy gloves, not a whit less ancient than the wig, which lay carefully folded up upon the table before him, and upon his legs were a pair of old leather spatter–dashes, clouted in twenty different places, and buttoned up all along the outside of his leg with brass buttons. He was consumedly grave and sparing of his talk, but every now and then a dry joke escaped him.

At the opposite side of the table sat another piece of antiquity, one Major Spratt,3 a thin, tall man, very phthisical, and addicted much to a dry cough. His face was adorned and set out with very large carbuncles, and he was more than half seas over in liquor. I understood he professed poetry, and often applied himself to rhyming, in which he imagined himself a very good artist. He gave us a specimen of his poetry in an epitaph, which he said he had composed upon one Purcell, a neighbour of his, lately dead; asked us if we did not think it excellent, and the best of that kind ever we heard. He repeated it ten times over with a ludicrous air and action. "Gentlemen," said he, "pray take notice now, give good attention. It is perhaps the concisest, wittiest, prettiest epigram or epitaph, call it what you will, that you ever heard.

Shall I get you pen and ink to write it down? Perhaps you may n't remember it else. It is highly worth your noting. Pray observe how it runs.

"Here lies John Purcell; and whether he be in heaven or in hell, Never a one of us all can tell."

This poet asked me very kindly how I did, and took me by the hand, tho' I never had seen him in my life before. He said he liked me for the sake of my name; told me he was himself nearly related to Colonel Hamilton 1 in the jerseys, son of the late Governour Hamilton' there. Then from one digression to another he told me that the coat he had upon his back was thirty years old. I believed him, for every button was as large as an ordinary turnip, the button–holes at least a quarter of a yard long, and the pocket holes just down at the skirts.

After some confused topsy–turvy conversation, the landlord sang a bawdy song, at which the grave parson–doctor got up, told us that was a language he did not understand, and therefore took his horse and rid away; but, in little more than half an hour or three quarters returned again and told us he had forgot his gloves, and had rid two miles of his way before he missed them. I was surprised at the old man's care of such a greasy bargain as these gloves. They were fit for nothing but to be wore by itchified persons under a course of sulphur, and I don't know but the doctor had lent them to some of his patients for that purpose, by which means they had imbibed such a quantity of grease. The landlord told me he was a man worth 5,000 pounds sterling, and had got it by frugality. I replied that this instance of the gloves was such a demonstration of carefulness that I wondered he was not worth twice as much.

At four o'clock I came to my lodging, and drank tea with Mrs. Hogg, and Mr. John Watts,' a Scots gentleman, came to pay me a visit. At five I went to the coffee–house, and there meeting with Mr. Dupeyster,2 he carried me to the tavern, where in a large room were convened a certain club of merry fellows. Among the rest was H –d, the same whom I extolled before for his art in touching the violin; but that indeed seemed to be his principal excellency. Other things he pretended to, but fell short. He affected being a wit and dealt much in pointed satire, but it was such base metal that the edge or point was soon turned when put to the proof. When anybody spoke to him, he seemed to give ear in such a careless manner as if he thought all discourse but his own trifling and insignificant. In short he was fit to shine nowhere, but among your good–natured men and ignorant blockheads. There was a necessity for the first to bear with the stupidity of his satire and for the others to admire his pseudosophia and quaintness of his speeches, and at the same time with their blocks to turn the edge and acuteness of his wit. He dealt much in proverbs, and made use of one which I thought pretty significant when well applied. It was *the devil to pay, and no pitch hot?* an interrogatory adage metaphorically derived from the manner of sailors, who pay their ships' bottoms with pitch. I backed it with *great cry and little wool, said the devil when he shore his hogs,* applicable enough to the ostentation and flutter he made with his learning.

There was in this company one Dr. McGraa, a pretended Scotsman, but by brogue a Teague. He had an affected way of curtsying instead of bowing when he entered a room. He put on a modest look, uncommon to his nation, spoke little, and when he went to speak leaned over the table and stretched out his neck and face, goose–like, as if he had been going to whisper you in the ear. When he drank to any in the company he would not speak, but kept bowing and bowing, sometimes for the space of a minute or two, till the person complimented either observed him of his own accord or was hunched into attention by his next neighbour, but it was hard to know whom he bowed to, upon account of his squinting.

However, when the liquor began to heat him a little, he talked at the rate of three [hundred?] words in a minute, and, sitting next me (he was very complaisant in his cups), he told me he had heard my name mentioned by some Marylanders, and asked me if I knew his uncle Grierson in Maryland. I returned his compliments in as civil a man nothing but waiting upon one another at our lodgings, but after all this complimentary farce and promises of serving and waiting were over, I could not but observe that none of us tools the trouble to inquire where the one or the other lodged. I never met with a man so wrapped up in himself as this fellow seemed to be, nor did I ever see a face where there was so much effrontery under a pretended mask of modesty.

There was, besides, another doctor in company, named Mann, doctor of a man–of–war. The best thing I saw about him was that he would drink nothing but water, but he eat lustily at supper, and nothing remarkable appeared in his discourse (which indeed was copious and insipid) but only an affected way he had of swearing by God at every two words; and by the motion of his hands at each time of swearing that polite and elegant oath, he would seem to let the company understand that he was no mean orator, and that the little oath was a very fine ornament to his oration.

But the most remarkable person in the whole company was one Wendall, a young gentleman from Boston. He entertained us mightily by playing on the violin the quickest tunes upon the highest keys, which he accompanied with his voice, so as even to drown the violin, with such nice shakings and gracings that I thought his voice outdid the instrument. I sat for some time immovable with surprise. The like I never heard, and the thing seemed to me next a miracle. The extent of his voice is impossible to describe or even to imagine unless by hearing him. The whole company were amazed that any person but a woman or eunuch could have such a pipe, and began to question his virility; but he swore that if the company pleased he would show a couple of as good witnesses as any man might wear. He then imitated several beasts, as dogs, cats, horses, and cows, and the cackling of poultry, and all to such perfection that nothing but nature could match it. When the landlord (a clumsy, sallow–faced fellow in a white jacket) came to receive his reckoning, our mimic's art struck and surprised him in such a manner that it fixed him quite, like one that had seen the Gorgon's head, and he might have passed for a statue done in white marble. He was so struck that the company might have gone away without paying and carried off all his silver tankards and spoons, and he never would have observed.

After being thus entertained I returned to my lodging at eleven o'clock.

Saturday, July 7th.–In the morning I waited upon Stephen Bayard, to whom my letters of credit were directed. He invited me to a Sunday's dinner with him. We heard news of a coasting vessel belonging to N. England taken by a French privateer in her passage betwixt Boston and Rhode Island. I writ to Annapolis by the post. I dined at Todd's, and went in the afternoon to see the French prizes in the harbour. Both of them were large ships about 300 tons burden,–the one Le Jupiter and the other Le Saint François Xavier. Warren, who took the St. Francis, has gained a great character. His praise is in everybody's mouth, and he has made a fine estate of the business. I went home at night, and shunned company.

Sunday, July 8th. –I spent the morning at home, and at one o'clock went to dine with Mr. Bayard. Among some other gentlemen there, was my old friend Dr. McGraa, who to–day seemed to have more talk and ostentation than usual, but he did not shine quite bright till he had drunk half a dozen glasses of wine after dinner. He spoke now in a very arbitrary tone, as if his opinion was to pass for an *ipse dixit.* He and I unhappily engaged in a dispute, which I was sorry for, it being dissonant to good manners before company, and what none but rank pedants will be guilty of. We were obliged to use hard physical terms, very discordant and disagreeable to ears not accustomed to them. I wanted much to drop it, but he kept teasing of me. I found my chap to be one of those learned bullies who by loud talking and an affected sneer seem to outshine all other men in parts of literature where the company are by no means proper judges, where for the most part the most impudent of the disputants passes for the most knowing man. The subject of this dispute was the effect which the moon has upon all fluids as well as the ocean, in a proportionable ratio, by the law of gravitation or her attractive power, and even upon the fluids in the vessels of animals. . . . He did not believe the moon had anything to do with us or our distempers, and said that such notions were only superstitious nonsense, wondering how I could give credit to any such stuff. We had a great deal of talk about attraction, condensation, gravitation, rarefaction, of all which I found he understood just as much as a goose; and when he began to show his ignorance of the mathematical and astronomical problems of the illustrious Newton, and blockishly resolve all my meaning into judicial astrology, I gave him up as an unintelligent, unintelligible, and consequently inflexible disputant, and the company being no judges of the thing, imagined, I suppose, that he had got the victory, which did not at all make me uneasy. He pretended to have travelled most countries in Europe, to have shared the favour and acquaintance of some foreign princes and grandees, and to have been at their tables; to be master of several European languages, tho' I found he could not speak good French, and he merely murdered the Latin. He said he had been very intimate with Professor Boerhaave and Dr. Astruc, and subjoined that he knew for certain that the majority of the Spanish bishops were Jews.

There was another doctor at dinner with us, who went away before this dispute began.

His name was Ascough. When he came first in, he told Mr. Bayard he would dine with him, provided he had no green pease for dinner. Mr. Bayard told hiln there were some, but that they should not come to table, upon which, with some entreaty, the doctor sat down, and eat pretty heartily of bacon, chickens, and veal; but just as he had begun upon his veal, the stupid negro wench, forgetting her orders to the contrary, produced the pease, at which the doctor began to stare and change colour in such a manner that I thought he would have been convulsed, but he started up and ran out of doors so fast that we could never throw salt on his tail again. Mr. Bayard was so angry that he had almost overset the table, but we had a good dish of pease by the bargain, which otherwise we should not have tasted. This was the oddest antipathy ever I was witness to. At night I went to Waghorn's, and found my company had delayed their setting off till Tuesday, so I returned home.

Monday, July 9th.–I waited upon Mr. Bayard this morning, and had letters of credit drawn upon Mr. Lechmere at Boston. I dined with Mr. M s and other company at Todd's, and went to tarry this night at the inn where my horses were, in order to set out to–morrow morning betimes on my journey for Boston. We heard news this day of an English vessel, laden with ammunition and bound for New England, being taken on the coast. I spent the evening at Waghorn's, where we had Mr. Wendall's company, who entertained us as before. We had among us this night our old friend Major Spratt, who now and then gave us an extempore rhyme. I retired to bed at twelve o'clock.

The people of New York, at the first appearance of a stranger, are seemingly civil and courteous, but this civility and complaisance soon relaxes if he be not either highly recommended or a good toaper. To drink stoutly with the Hungarian Club, who are all bumper men, is the readiest way for a stranger to recommend himself, and a set among them are very fond of making a stranger drunk. To talk bawdy and to have a knack at punning passes among some there for good sterling wit. Governour Clinton himself is a jolly toaper and gives good example, and for that one quality is esteemed among these dons.

The staple of New York is bread flour and skins. It is a very rich place, but it is not so cheap living here as at Philadelphia. They have very bad water in the city, most of it being hard and brackish. Ever since the negro conspiracy, certain people have been appointed to sell water in the streets, which they carry on a sledge in great casks and bring it from the best springs about the city, for it was when the negroes went for tea water that they held their cabals and consultations, and therefore they have a law now that no negro shall be seen upon the streets without a lanthorn after dark.

In this city are a mayor, recorder, aldermen, and common council. The government is under the English law, but the chief places are possessed by Dutchmen, they composing the best part of the House of Assembly. The Dutch were the first settlers of this Province, which is very large and extensive, the States of Holland having purchased the country of one Hudson, who pretended first to have discovered it, but they at last exchanged it with the English for Saranam, and ever since there have been a great number of Dutch here, tho' now their language and customs begin pretty much to wear out, and would very soon die were it not for a parcel of Dutch domines here, who, in the education of their children, endeavour to preserve the Dutch customs as much as possible. There is as much jarring here betwixt the powers of the Legislature as in any of the other American Provinces.

They have a diversion here very common, which is the barbecuing of a turtle, to which sport the chief gentry in town commonly go once or twice a week.

There are a great many handsome women in this city. They appear much more in public than at Philadelphia. It is customary here to ride thro' the street in light chairs. When the ladies walk the streets in the daytime they commonly use umbrellas, prettily adorned with feathers and painted.

There are two coffee–houses in this city, and the northern and southern posts go and come here once a week. I was tired of nothing here but their excessive drinking, for in this place you may have the best of company and conversation as well as at Philadelphia.

YORK FERRY–LONG ISLAND–JAMAICA

Tuesday July 10th.–Early in the morning we got up, and after preparing all our baggage, Messrs. Parker, Laughton, and I mounted horse, and crossed the ferry at seven o'clock over to Long Island. After a tedious passage and being detained some time at Baker's, we arrived a quarter after ten at Jamaica, a small town upon Long Island, just bordering upon Hampstead Plain. It is about half a mile long; the houses sparse. There are in it one Presbyterian meeting, one English and one Dutch church. The Dutch church is built in the shape of an octagon, being a wooden structure. We stopped there at the sign of the Sun, and paid dear for our breakfast, which was bread and mouldy cheese, stale beer, and sour cider.

HAMPSTEAD

WE set out again and arrived at Hampstead, a very scattered town, standing upon the great plain to which it gives name. We put up here at one Peters's, at the sign of Guy of Warwick, where we dined with a company that had come there before us, and were travelling southward. There was a pretty girl here, with whom Parker was mightily taken, and would fain have staid that night. This girl had intermitting fevers. Parker pretended to be a doctor, and swore he could cure her if she would submit to his directions. With difficulty we persuaded Parker to mount horse.

At four o'clock, going across this great plain, we could see almost as good a horizon round us as when one is at sea, and in some places of the plain, the latitude might be taken by observation at noonday. It is about sixteen miles long. The ground is hard and gravelly; the road very smooth but indistinct, and intersected by several other roads, which make it difficult for a stranger to find the way. There is nothing but long grass grows upon this plain, only in some particular spots small oak brush, not above a foot high. Near Hampstead there are several pretty winding brooks that run thro'this plain.

We lost our way here, and blundered about a great while. At last we spied a woman and two men at some distance. We rid up towards them to inquire, but they were too wild to be spoke with, running over the plain as fast as wild bucks upon the mountains. Just after we came out of the plain and stink into the woods, we found a boy lurking behind a bush. We wanted to inquire the way of him, but, as soon as we spoke, the game was started and away he ran.

HUNTINGTON

WE arrived at Huntington at eight o'clock at night, where we put up at one Flat's, at the sign of the Half–moon and Heart. This Flat is an Irishman. We had no sooner sat down, when there came in a band of the town politicians in short jackets and trousers, being probably curious to know who them strangers were who had newly arrived in town. Among the rest was a fellow with a worsted cap and great black fists. They styled him doctor. Flat told me he had been a shoemaker in town, and was a notable fellow at his trade, but happening two years ago to cure an old woman of a pestilent mortal disease, he thereby acquired the character of a physician, was applied to from all quarters, and finding the practice of physic a more profitable business than cobbling, he laid aside his awls and leather, got himself some gallipots, and instead of cobbling of soales fell to cobbling of human bodies. At supper our landlord was very merry, and very much given to rhyming.

There were three buxom girls in this house, who served us at supper, to whom Mr. Parker made strenuous courtship. One was an Indian girl named Phoebe; the other two were Lucretia and Betty; but Betty was the topbeauty of the three.

Wednesday, July 11th.–We left Huntington at half an hour after six in the morning, and after riding five miles stony road, we breakfasted at a house upon the road, at the sign of Bacchus. Then proceeding ten or eleven miles f arther, we forded Smithtown River, otherwise called by the Indians Missaque. We baited our horses at a tavern where there was a deaf landlady. After half an hour's rest we mounted horse again, and rid some miles thro' some very barren, unequal, and stony land. We saw the mouth of Smithtown River running into the sound, thro' some broken sandy beaches about eight miles to our left hand N. N. W., and about twenty–four miles farther to the northward, the coast of the main of New England or the Province of Connecticut.

BROOKHAVEN, OR SETOQUET

We arrived at a scattered town called Brookhaven, or by the Indians Setoquet, about two o'clock afternoon, and dined at one Buchanan's there.

Brookhaven is a small scattered village, standing upon barren rocky land near the sea. In this town is a small windmill for sawing of plank, and a wooden church with a small steeple.

At about fifty miles' distance from this town eastward is a settlement of Indians, upon a sandy point, which makes the south fork of the island, and runs out a long narrow promontory into the sea, almost as far as Block Island.

While we were at Buchanan's an old fellow named Smith called at the house. He said he was a–travelling to York, to get a license or commission from the Governour to go a–privateering, and swore he would not be under any commander, but would be chief man himself. He showed us several antic tricks, such as jumping half a foot high upon his bum, without touching the floor with any other part of his body. Then he turned and did the same upon his belly. Then he stood upright upon his head. He told us he was seventy–five years of age and swore damn his old shoes if any man in America could do the like. He asked me whence I came and whither I went. I answered him I came from Calliphurnia and was going to Lanthern Land. He swore damn his old shoes again if he had not been a sailor all his life long and yet never had heard of such places. Mr. Parker made him believe that he was a captain of a privateer, and for a mug of cider made him engage to go on board of him upon Friday next, promising to make him his lieutenant, for nothing else would satisfy the old fellow. The old chap was mightily elevated at this and damned his old shoes twenty times over. At last he wanted to borrow a little advance money of Parker, which when he found he could not obtain, he drank up his cider, and swore he would not go.

We took horse again at half an hour after five o'clock, and had scarce got a mile from Brookhaven when we lost our way, but were directed right again by a man whom we met. After riding ten miles thro' woods and marshes, in which we were pestered with mosquitoes, we arrived at eight o'clock at night at one Brewster's, where we put up for all night, and in this house we could get nothing either to eat or drink, and so were obliged to go to bed fasting or supperless. I was conducted upstairs to a large chamber. The people in this house seemed to be quite savage and rude.

Thursday, July 12th.–When I waked this morning I found two beds in the room, besides that in which I lay, in one of which lay two great hulking fellows, with long black beards, having their own hair, and not so much as half a nightcap betwixt both them. I took them for weavers, not only from their greasy appearance, but because I observed a weaver's loom at each side of the room. In the other bed was a raw–boned boy, who, with the two lubbers, huddled on his clothes, and went reeling downstairs, making as much noise as three horses.

We set out from this desolate place at six o'clock, and rid sixteen miles thro' very barren and waste land. Here we passed thro' a plain of six or eight miles long, where was nothing but oak brush or bushes, two feet high, very thick, and replenished with acorns; and thinly scattered over the plain were several old naked pines at about two or three hundred feet's distance one from another, most of them decayed and broken. In all this way we met not one living soul, nor saw any house but one in ruins. Some of the inhabitants here call this place the Desert of Arabia. It is very much infected with mosquitoes. We breakfasted at one Fanning's. Near his house stands the County Court–house, a decayed wooden building, and close by his door runs a small rivulet into an arm of the sea about twenty miles' distance, which makes that division of the eastern end of Long Island called the Fork.

SOUTH HOLD

This day was rainy, but we took horse and rid ten miles farther to one Hubbard's, where we rested half an hour, then proceeded eight miles farther to the town of Southhold, near which the road is level, firm, and pleasant, and in the neighborhood are a great many windmills. The houses are pretty thick along the road here. We put up at one Mrs. Moore's in Southhold. In her house appeared nothing but industry. She and her grand–daughters were busied in carding and spinning of wool. Messieurs Parker and Laughton were very much disposed to sleep. We ordered some eggs for dinner and some chickens. Mrs. Moore asked us if we would have bacon fried with our eggs; we told her no. After dinner we sent to inquire for a boat to cross the Sound.

At night the house was crowded with a company of patched coats and tattered jackets, and consequently the conversation consisted chiefly in damn ye, Jack; and here's to you, Tom. A comical old fellow among the rest asked me if I had come from the new country.

His name he told me was Cleveland, and he was originally of Scots parentage. I told him then his genuine name must be Cleland. We asked him what entertainment we could have at the oyster pond, where we designed to take boat to cross ye Sound. "Why truly," said he, "if you would eat such things as we Gentiles do, you may live very well, but as your law forbids you to eat swine's flesh your living will be but indifferent." Parker laughed, and asked him if he took us for Jews or Mahometans. He replied: "Gentlemen, I ask pardon, but the landlady informed me you were Jews." This notion proceeded from our refusing of bacon to our eggs at dinner.

While we were at supper there came in a peddler with his pack, along with one Doctor Hull, a practitioner of physick in the town. We were told that this doctor was a man of great learning, and very much of a gentleman. The peddler went to show him some linen by candle–light, and told him very ingenuously that now he would be upon honour with him and recommend to him the best of his wares, and as to the price he would let him know the highest and lowest at one word, and would not bate one penny of six shillings a yard. There passed some learned conversation betwixt this doctor and peddler, in which the doctor made it plain that the lawyers, clergy, and doctors tricked the rest of mankind out of the best part of their substance, and made them pay well for doing of nothing. But the peddler stood up mightily for the honour of his own profession, and affirmed that they made as good a hand of it as any cheat among them all; "but then," added he, "you have something to handle for your money, good or bad, as it happens." We left this company at nine o'clock at night, and went upstairs to bed, all in one chamber.

OYSTER POND

Friday, July 13th.–We took horse after six in the morning and rid five or six miles close by the Sound till we came to one Brown's, who was to give us passage in his boat. Then we proceeded seven miles farther, and stopped at one King's to wait the tide when Brown's boat was to fall down the river, to take us in. The family at King's were all busy in preparing dinner, the provision for which chiefly consisted in garden stuff. Here we saw some handsome country girls, one of whom wore a perpetual smile in her face, and prepared the chocolate for our breakfast. She presently captivated Parker, who was apt to take flame upon all occasions. After breakfast for pastime we read Quevedo's visions, and at one o'clock dined with the family upon fat pork and green pease. At two o'clock we observed the boat falling down the river, and having provided ourselves with a store of bread and cheese and some rum and sugar, in case of being detained upon the water, that part of the Sound which we had to cross being eighteen miles broad, we put our horses on board ten minutes before three, and set sail with a fair wind from the Oyster Pond.

SOUND

At three o'clock we crossed the Gut, a rapid current, betwixt the main of Long Island and Shelter Island, caused by the tides.

SHELTER ISLAND– GARDINER'S ISLAND

At a quarter after three, we cleared Shelter Island, larboard, upon our weather bow. Gardiner's Island bore east by north, starboard, about three leagues' distance. This island is in the possession of one man, and takes its name from him. It had been a prey to the French privateers in Queen Anne's war, who used to land upon it and plunder the family and tenants of their stock and provisions, the island lying very bleak upon the ocean, just at the easternmost entry of the Sound, betwixt Long Island and the main of Connecticut.

FISHER'S ISLAND–TWO–TREE ISLAND

A little to the northward of this lies Fisher's Island, and about three or four leagues' distance upon our larboard we saw a small island called Two–tree Island, because they say there are only two trees upon it, which are of a particular kind of wood, which nobody there can give a name to, nor are such trees to be seen anywhere else in the country.

CONNECTICUT GOVERNMENT–NEW LONDON

WE arrived in the harbour at New London at half an hour after six, and put up at Duchand's at the sign of the Anchor. The town of New London is irregularly built along the water side, in length about a mile. There is in it one Presbyterian meeting and one church.

This just such another desolate, extensive town as Annapolis in Maryland, the houses being mostly wood. The inhabitants were alarmed this night at a sloop that appeared to be rowing up into the harbour, they having heard a little before a firing of guns out in the Sound, and seen one vessel, as they thought, give chase to another. There was a strange clamour and crowd in the street, chiefly of women. The country station sloop lay in the harbour, who, when she was within shot, sent her a salute; first one gun, sharp shot, but the advancing sloop did not strike; then she bestowed upon her another, resolving next to proceed to a volley; but at the second shot, which whistled thro' her rigging, she struck and made answer that it was one Captain Trueman from Antigua. Then the people's fears were over, for they imagined it was old Morpang, the French rover, who in former times used to plunder these parts when he wanted provision.

NEW LONDON FERRY

Saturday, July 14th.–We departed New London at seven o'clock in the morning, crossing the ferry, and rid eight miles thro' a very stony rough road, where the stones upon each hand of us seemed as large as houses, and the way itself a mere rock.

STONINGTON

This is properly enough called Stonington. We breakfasted at one Major Williams's, and proceeded ten miles farther to Thomson's, where we baited our horses. Here we met one Captain Noise, a dealer in cattle, whose name and character seemed pretty well to agree, for he talked very loud, and joaked and laughed heartily at nothing.

RHODE ISLAND AND PROVIDENCE GOVERNMENT

The landlady here was a queer old woman, an enormous heap of fat. She had some daughters and maids, whom she called by comical names. There were Thankful, Charity, Patience, Comfort, Hope, etc.

Upon the road here stands a house belonging to an Indian King named George, commonly called King George's house or palace. He possesses twenty or thirty thousand acres of very fine level land round this house, upon which he has many tenants, and has of his own a good stock of horses and other cattle. The King lives after the English mode. His subjects have lost their own government policy and laws, and are servants or vassals to the English here. His queen goes in a high modish dress in her silks, hoops, stays, and dresses like an Englishwoman. He educates his children to the *belles lettres* and is himself a very complaisant, mannerly man. We payed him a visit, and he treated us with a glass of good wine.

We dined at one Hill's, and going from thence at four o'clock, and travelling thro' twelve miles more of stony, rough road, we passed by an oldfashioned wooden house at the end of a lane, darkened and shaded over with a thick grove of tall trees. This appeared to me very romantic, and brought into my mind some romantic descriptions of rural scenes in Spenser's *Faerie Queene.*

SUGAR LOAF

About a quarter of a mile farther, at the end of a lane, is a little hill, that rises up in a conical form and is therefore called the Sugar Loaf. The fencing here is all stone. We could see to our right hand the ocean and part of the Sound, the long point of Long Island called Montague Block Island, and at a good distance, behind an island called Conannicut, part of Rhode Island.

At six o'clock we arrived at a village called Tower Hill or South Kingstown. It lies near the sea. All round here the country is high, hilly, and rocky; few woods and these dwarfish. You have a large, extensive prospect from here, both to the sea and landward. We put up at the house of one Case in Kingstown, who keeps a pretty good house, is a talkative, prating man, and would have everybody know that he keeps the best public house in the country. We heard news of some prizes brought into Newport by the Rhode Island privateers, and among the rest a large Spanish snow, with no loading, but 30,000 pounds' value, New England money, in silver, which is 5,000 pounds sterling.

Sunday, July 15th.–We tarried at Case's all this day, it being unlawful here to travel upon Sunday, or, as they term it, Sabbath day (Sunday being a pagan name). We loitered about all the forenoon, having nothing to do and no books to read, except it was a curious History of the Nine Worthies (which we found in Case's library), a book worthy of that worthy author Mr. Burton, the diligent compiler and historian of Grub Street. Case was mightily offended by Mr. Laughton for singing and whistling, telling him that he ought not so to profane the sabbath. Laughton swore that he had forgot what day it was, but Case was still more offended at his swearing, and left us in bad humour.

This day was bleak and stormy, the wind being at east by north. I diverted myself by looking at the coasting sloops passing up and down by Connannicut Point, which runs out here, much like Greenberry's near Annapolis, but is quite bare, rocky, and barren. Upon it the tide beats with great violence, so as to raise a white foam a great way round it. We dined at three o'clock, and after dinner walked out to see our horses in the pasture, where my gray, having laid himself down at full length to sleep, I imagined at a distance that he was dead; but throwing a stone at him he started up and got to his heels. We viewed the sea from a high rock, where we could see the spray beating with violence over the tops of the rocks upon the coast, and below us, of three or four miles' extent, a pleasant green meadow, thro' the middle of which ran a pretty winding river. Most of the country round is open, hilly, and rocky, and upon the rocks there is a great deal of spar, or substance like white marble, but in very small pieces.

We returned home at six o'clock, and had a rambling conversation with Case and a certain traveller upon different subjects. There came to the house at night a Rhode Island colonel (for in this country there is great plenty of colonels, captains, and majors), who diverted us with some stories about the Newlightmen. There are a great many Seventhdaymen here, who keep Saturday instead of Sunday, and so go to work when others go to church. Most of the people here begin their Sunday upon Saturday night after sunset, and end it upon Sunday at sunset, when they go to any kind of recreation or work upon other days lawful.

After a light supper of bread and milk, we went to bed.

NARAGANTSET FERRY–DUTCH ISLAND

Monday, July 16th.–We set off from Case's at half an hour after six in the morning, and crossed Conannicut Ferry or Naragantset betwixt eight and nine o'clock.

RHODE ISLAND FERRY

There is a small island lies betwixt the main and Conannicut, called Dutch Island, because the Dutch first took possession of it. We crossed the other ferry to Newport, upon Rhode Island, a little after ten o'clock, and had a very heavy rain all the passage.

DUMPLIN'S–ROSE ISLAND

THERE are some rocks there called the Dumplin's, and a little above a small island called Rose Island, upon which there is one tree. Here you have very pretty views and prospects from the mixture of land and water. As we stepped into the ferry boat there were some stones lay in her bottom, which obstructed the horses getting in. Dromo desired the skipper to "trow away his stones, de horse be better ballast." "No," says the fellow, "I cannot part with my stones yet; they will serve for a good use at another time."

We arrived at Newport at 12 o'clock. Rhode Island is a pleasant, open spot of land, being an entire garden of farms, twelve or thirteen miles long and four or five miles broad at its broadest part. The town Newport is about a mile long, lying pretty near north and south. It stands upon a very level spot of ground, and consists of one street, narrow, but so straight that, standing at one end of it, you may see to the other. It is just close upon the water. There are several lanes going from this street, on both sides. Those to the landward are some of them pretty long and broad. There is one large Market–house, near the south end of the main street. The Town–house stands a little above this Market–house, away from the water, and is a handsome brick edifice, lately built, having a cupola at top. There is besides in this town two Presbyterian meetings, one large Quaker meeting, one Anabaptist, and one Church of England.' The church has a very fine organ in it, and there is a publick clock upon the steeple as also upon the front of the Town–house. The fort' is a square building of brick and stone, standing upon a small island, which makes the harbour. This place is famous for privateering, and they had about this time brought in several prizes, among which was a large Spanish snow near aoo tons burden, which I saw in the harbour, with her bowsprit shot off.

This town is as remarkable for pretty women as Albany is for ugly ones, many of whom one may see sitting in the shops in passing along the street. I dined at a tavern kept by one Nicolls at the sign of the White Horse, where I had put up my horses, and in the afternoon, Dr. Moffatt, an old acquaintance and schoolfellow of mine, led me a course thro' the town. He carried me to see one Feake,2 a painter, the most extraordinary genius ever I knew, for he does pictures tolerably well by the force of genius, having never had any teaching. I saw a large table of the judgment of Hercules, copied by him from a frontispiece of the Earl of Shaftesbury's, which I thought very well done. This man had exactly the phiz of a painter, having a long pale face, sharp nose, large eyes, with which he looked upon you steadfastly,–long curled black hair, a delicate white hand, and long fingers.

I went with Moffatt in the evening to Dr.Keith's, another countryman and acquaintance, where we spent the evening very agreeably in the company of one Dr. Brett,' a very facetious old man. I soon found that Keith passed for a man of great gallantry here, being frequently visited by the young ladies in town, who are generally very airy and frolicsome. He showed me a drawer full of the trophies of the fair, which he called his cabinet of curiosities. They consisted of torn fans, fragments of gloves, whims, snuff–boxes, girdles, apronstrings, laced shoes and shoe–heels, pin–cushions, hussifs, and a deal of other such trumpery. I lay this night at Dr. Moffatt's lodging.

Tuesday, July 17th.–I breakfasted with Dr. Moffatt, and had recommendatory letters of him to some of the fraternity in Boston. I went with the Doctor at ten o'clock to see a house about half a mile out of town, built lately by one Captain Mallbone, a substantial trader there. It is the largest and most magnificent dwelling–house I have seen in America. It is built entirely of hewn stone of a reddish colour; the sides of the windows and corner–stones of the house being painted like white marble. It is three stories high, and the rooms are spacious and magnificent. There is a large lanthern or cupola on the roof, which is covered with sheet lead. The whole staircase, which is very spacious and large, is done with mahogany wood. This house makes a grand show at a distance, but is not extraordinary for the architecture, being a clumsy Dutch model. Round it are pretty gardens and terraces, with canals and basins for water, from whence you have a delightful view of the town and harbour of Newport, with the shipping lying there.

When Mr. Parker and Laughton came up, we proceeded on our journey, riding along the island a broad and even road, where our eyes were entertained with various beautiful prospects of the continent, islands, and water. From some high places we could see Block Island to the westward. We dined at Burden's, a Quaker, who keeps the ferry, where we had good entertainment, and met with one Mr. Lee, a proprietor in some iron works near Boston. We crossed the ferry at four o'clock, and rid some miles of stony, unequal road.

MASSACHUSETTS PROVINCE–MOUNT HOPE

As we entered the Province of the Massachusetts Bay, upon the left hand we saw a hill called Mount Hope, formerly the stronghold or refuge of an Indian king named Philip, who held the place a long time against the first settlers, and used to be very troublesome by making excursions.

BRISTOL

We passed thro' Bristol, a small trading town, laid out in the same manner as Philadelphia, about three o'clock. We crossed another little ferry at five o'clock, and baited at one Hunt's, then riding ten miles farther we parted with Mr. Lee, and lay that night at one Slake's, at the sign of the White Horse.

Wednesday, July 28th.–We set out a little after six in the morning, breakfasted at Mann's,, and from thence went ten miles farther to Robins's,' where we parted. We were resolved to dine at Dedham, but were scarce got upon our horses when we were met by a company of gentlemen, who being acquaintances of Parker and Laughton, they persuaded us to turn back to Robins's again. There was in this company one Coffin,' who inquired after my brother in Maryland, and told me he had once been a patient of his when at Benedict Town upon Patuxent, about sixteen or seventeen years ago.

In this house I and my company were taken for peddlers. There happened to be a peddler there selling some wares, who saw me open my portmanteau and sort some bundles and packets of letters. He mistook my portmanteau for a pack, for it is not very customary here to ride with such implements, and so would have chaffered with me for some goods.

While we were at dinner one Mr. Lightfoot came in, to whom I had a recommendatory letter. This Lightfoot is a gentleman of a regular education, having been brought up at Oxford in England, a man of good humour and excellent sense. He had upon his head, when he entered the company, a straw hat dyed black, but no wig. He told us that he always rode in this trim in hot weather, but that among the country people he had been taken for a French spy, upon account of the oddity of his dress. He said he had heard a grand laugh as he passed by, and guessing that there were some Boston people in the company he was induced to call in. Then he pulled about two pounds of black rye bread out of his pocket, and told us that he thought perhaps he might come to some places upon the road where there might be a scarcity of fine bread, and therefore had provided himself.

We had news here of the French having, along with the Cape Sable and St. John Indians, made an attack upon Annapolis Royal, and that they had killed all their cattle and several men there, and burnt down all the houses in the town, so that the inhabitants, in the utmost distress, were obliged to betake themselves to the fort, where they were scanty of provisions and ready to surrender, when Captain Ting, master of the Boston galley, came seasonably to their assistance with a reinforcement of men and a fresh supply of provisions, and as soon as the enemy heard his guns they fled into the woods. This Ting has gained a great character here for his conduct and courage.

DEDHAM

We parted from Robins's a little after three, and betwixt five and six arrived at Dedham, a village within eleven miles of Boston, where we rested a little and drank some punch. Lightfoot had a scolding bout here with one Betty, the landlady's daughter, for secreting one of our lemons, and was obliged to vent a deal of billingsgate, and swear a string of lusty oaths, before he could recover it again. He told me that this place was the most sharping country ever I was in, and that this little peddling trick was only the beginning of it, and nothing to what I should experience if I stayed but some weeks there. We took horse at half an hour after six, and passed several pretty country boxes at three or four miles' distance from Boston, belonging to gentlemen in the town.

BLUE HILLS

At thirteen miles' distance from Boston is a range of hills, called the Blue Hills, upon the top of one of which a gentleman has built a country house, where there is a very extensive view. A quarter before eight we arrived in Boston.

BOSTON

There I put my horses at one Barker's' and took lodging at Mrs. Guneau's, a Frenchwoman, at the back of the Almshouse, near Beacon Hill, a very pleasant part of the town, situated high and well aired. My landlady and I conversed about two hours. She informed me that one Mr. Hughes, a merchant, that lately had been in Maryland, lodged at her house, which I was glad to hear, having had some small acquaintance with him. My landlady was a Frenchwoman, and had much of the humour of that nation, a deal of talk and a deal of action. I went to bed at eleven o'clock.

Thursday, July 19th.–I got up half an hour after five in the morning, and after breakfast I took a turn in the garden with Mr. Hughes, from whence we had a view of the whole town of Boston, and the peninsula upon which it stands. The neck which joins this peninsula to the land is situated southwest from the town, and at low water is not above thirty or forty paces broad, and is so flat and level that in high tides it is sometimes overflowed. The town is built upon the south and southeast side of the peninsula and is about two miles in length, extending from the neck of the peninsula northward to that place called North End, as that extremity of the town next the neck is called South End. Behind the town are several pleasant plains, and on the west side of the peninsula are three hills in a range, upon the highest of which is placed a long beacon pole. To the northward over the water is situated a pretty large town called Charlestown. We could see a great many islands out in the bay, upon one of which, about three miles from town, stands the Castle, a strong fortification, that guards the entry of the harbour upon the most extreme island. About twelve miles out is the Lighthouse,' a high building of stone in form of a pillar, upon the top of which every night is kept a light to guide ships into the harbour. When a snow, brig, sloop, or schooner appears out at sea they hoist a pinnace upon the flag–staff in the Castle; if a ship, they display a flag.

At twelve o'clock I waited upon Mr. Hooper, one of the ministers in Boston, and from thence went to Mr. Lechmere's,4 the surveyor's, to whom my letters of credit were directed. From his house I went to the Change, a place of public rendezvous. Here is a great building called the Townhouse,' about 125 feet long and forty feet broad. The lower chamber of this house, called the Change, is all one apartment, the roof of which is supported all along the middle with a row of wooden pillars, about twenty–five feet high. Upon Change I met Mr. Hutchinson and Captain Wendall, to whom I delivered letters. I went down to view the Long Wharf. This runs in a direct line with a broad street called King's Street, and is carried into the water pretty near a quarter of a mile. Upon one side of this wharf all along, there is a range of wooden houses, and close by the wharf lies a very numerous shipping. I dined at

Withered's, a tavern at the Change, and there heard news of the magazines at Placentia being blown up.

In the afternoon about six o'clock, Messrs. Parker and Laughton called at my lodging, and with them I took a tour round the north end of the town, and to the waterside, after which we went to a club at Withered's, where there was a pot–bellied doctor president. This man was as round as a ball, about five feet high, and pretended to be very knowing in politicks. He was a Frenchman by birth, and I understood he was by trade a usurer, letting out money at ten per cent. I left this club at ten o'clock and went home.

Friday, July loth. –I got up pretty early and took a turn in the garden. At eleven o'clock I went abroad with Mr. Hughes, and after taking a walk to the waterside we went to Change at twelve o'clock, where I delivered several letters. I saw at Change some Frenchmen, officers of the flag of truce, with prisoners for exchange from Canso, and of the privateer taken by Captain Ting. They were very loquacious, after the manner of their nation, and their discourse for the most part was interlaced with oaths and smut. At two o'clock Mr. Hughes and I dined with Mr. Hooper, where we had some agreeable conversation. I came home in the afternoon, and writ some letters to go by the ships to Great Britain.

Saturday, July first.–I rose later than usual this morning, and breakfasted with Mrs. Guneau and her daughter, the latter a passably handsome girl, nothing of the French spirit in her, but rather too grave and sedate. Near twelve o'clock I walked out with Mr. Hughes, and went to Change, where, after attending some time, and observing a variety of comical phizes, I encountered Captain Wendall, who pointed out Dr. Douglass 1 and Mr. Arbuthnot 2 to me, to whom I delivered letters.

I was invited to dine with Captain Irvin,' upon salt codfish, which here is a common Saturday dinner, being elegantly dressed with a sauce of butter and eggs. In our company here was one Captain Petty, a very hard–favored man, a Scotsman by birth, humpbacked, and the tallest humpy ever I saw, being six feet high at least. There was one Perkins, a little round–faced man, a trader in the place. The discourse turned chiefly upon commerce and trade, and thro' the whole of it I could discover a vein of that subtlety and acuteness so peculiar to a New England genius. Mr. Arbuthnot and I had some disputes concerning some particular High Church maxims, but as I looked upon the promoters and favourers of these doctrines to be every whit as absurd and silly as the doctrines themselves, and adapted only for weak people, so I thought all argumentation was thrown away upon them, and therefore I dropped the dispute, for, as I was a stranger, I cared not, for the sake of such damned trifles, to procure the odium or ill will of any person in the place. After dinner I went home and slept till the evening, the weather being pretty hot, and I having drunk too much wine, it made me heavy.

Sunday, July 22d.–After breakfast I went with Mr. Hughes to Hooper's meeting,' where we heard a very good discourse, and saw a genteel congregation. The ladies were most of them in high dress. This meeting–house is a handsome new wooden building, with a huge spire or steeple at the north end of it. The pulpit is large and neat, with a large sounding–board, supported at each end with pilasters of the Doric order, fluted, and behind it there is a high arched door, over which hangs a green curtain.

The pulpit cushion is of green velvet, and all the windows in the meeting are mounted with green curtains.

After dismissing I went to Change, and returning from thence dined with Mr. Lechmere. There was a lady at table of a very masculine make, but dressed fine *à la mode.*

She did not appear till dinner was almost over, pretending she could not endure the smell of the victuals, and was every now and then lugging out her sal volatile and Hungary water, but this I observed was only a modish air, for she made a shift betwixt times to swallow down as much beef and pudding as anybody at the table; in short her teeth went as fast as her tongue, and the motion of both was perpetual.

After dinner I went to the English chapel with Mr. Lechmere, and heard a small organ played by an indifferent organist. A certain pedantic Irishman preached to us, who had much of the brogue. He gave us rather a philosophical lecture than a sermon, and seemed to be one of those conceited prigs who are fond of spreading out to its full extent all that superficial physical knowledge which they have acquired more by hearsay than by application or study; but of all places the pulpit is the most improper for the ostentatious of this sort; the language and phraseology of which sacred rostrum ought to be as plain to the ploughman as the scholar. We had a load of impertinence from him about the specific gravity of air and water, the exhalation of vapours, the expansion and condensation of clouds, the operation of distillation, and the chemistry of nature. It fine it was but a very puerile physical lecture, and no sermon at all.

There sat some Indians in a pew near me who stank so that they had almost made me turn up my dinner. They made a profound reverence to the parson when he finished; the men bowed, and the squaws curtsied.

After dinner I writ a letter for Annapolis and drank tea with Mrs. Guneau and some ladies.

Monday, July 23rd.–This morning I walked abroad with Mr. Hughes, and passed over the dam at the reservoir' to the north end of the town. We surveyed the ships a–building upon the stocks, and went to see the new battery, a building of wood, just at the entry of that inlet of water that runs up towards Charlestown. This new battery mounts about fourteen or fifteen great guns, and facing the bay it runs out about fifty paces into the water. From thence we went and surveyed the merchants' warehouses, which stand all along the waterside.

We next viewed the new Market–house,' an elegant building of brick, with a cupola on the top, in length about 130 feet, in breadth betwixt 4o and 5o. This was built at the proper expense of one Funell, a substantial merchant of this place, lately dead, and presented by him to the public. It is called by the name of Funell Hall, and stands near a little inlet of water, called the Town dock, over which, a little below the Market–house, is a wooden drawbridge that turns upon hinges that small vessels may pass and lie above it. In low tides this inlet is a very stinking puddle.

At nine o'clock we finished our tour, and came home sharp–set for breakfast. At eleven o'clock Mr. Vans' came to visit me, and invited me to dine with him upon Tuesday. I went to Withered's at twelve o'clock, and from thence went to dine with Captain Wendall, where were some officers that had belonged to the garrison at Canso, and had been there when the place was taken by the French. They were brought to Boston by Captain Mangeau in the flag of truce. After dinner Captain Mangeau himself came in, who spoke such broken English that I understood his French much better. In the afternoon I called at Mr. Hooper's and agreed to go to Cambridge with him upon Wednesday.

Tuesday, July 24th.–I received this day a letter from Dr. Moffatt at Newport, Rhode Island, and answered the same by the opportunity of Mr. Hughes, who went there this day. Dr. Douglass paid me a short visit in the morning, and at twelve o'clock I went to Change, where I saw Mr. Vans, who carried me to dine with him.

Mr. Vans himself and his whole family I found to be great admirers of the New Light doctrines and scheme. His wife is a strenuous Whitfieldian. The word *carnal* was much used in our table talk, which seems to be a favorite word of the fair sex of that persuasion. There was one at table whom Mr. Vans called brother, who spoke very little, but had the most solemn puritanic countenance ever I had seen. The discourse chiefly turned upon religion, but the strain of it was so enthusiastic that I thought fit only to be a hearer.

After dinner I went with Mr. Vans to an auction of books in King street, where the auctioneer, a young fellow, was very witty in his way. "This book," says he, "gentlemen, must be valuable. Here you have everything concerning popes, cardinals, anti–christ, and the devil. Here, gentlemen, you have *Tacitus*, that elegant historian. He gives you an account of that good and pious person, Nero, who loved his mother and kindred so well that he sucked their very blood." The books that sold best at this auction, while I was there, were *Pamela, Antipamela, The Fortunate Maid*, Ovid's *Art o f Love and The Marrow o f Modern Divinity.*

We were called to the windows in the auction room by a noise in the street, which was occasioned by a parade of Indian chiefs marching up the street with Colonel Wendall. The fellows had all laced hats, and some of them laced matchcoats and ruffled shirts, and a multitude of the *plebs* of their own complexion followed them. This was one Henrique,1 and some other of the chiefs of the Mohooks, who had been deputed to treat with the eastern Indians bordering upon New England. This Hen rique is a bold, intrepid fellow. When he first arrived at the place of rendezvous, none of the eastern chiefs were come. However, he expressed himself to the commons to this purpose: "We the Mohooks," said he, "are your fathers, and you our children. If you are dutiful and obedient, if you brighten the chain with the English our friends, and take up the hatchet against the French our enemies, we will defend and protect you, but otherwise if you are disobedient and rebel you shall die, every man, woman, and child of you, and that by our hands. We will cut you off from the earth, as an ox licketh up the grass." To this answer that what he said was just. As for their parts they would do their best to keep their end of the house in order; but their house was a very long house, one end of it was light and the other dark, because having no doors or windows the sun could not shine in upon them. (By the dark end they meant the St. John and Cape Sable Indians of the same nation with them, but in the French interest.) In the light end they knew what they were a–doing, but nobody could see in the dark.

However, they would strike a light, and if possible discover its most secret corners. "It is true you are our fathers, and our lives depend upon you. We will always be dutiful, as we have hitherto been, for we have cleared a road all the way to Albany betwixt us and you, having cut away every tree and bush, that there might be no obstruction. You, our fathers, are like a porcupine full of prickles, to wound such as offend you; we, your children, are like little babes, whom you have put into cradles and rocked asleep." While they delivered this answer they appeared very much frightened, and in the meantime one Lewis, an eastern chief, came upon the field, who seemed to reprove Henrique for delivering his embassy to the common people while none of the chiefs were by, telling him it was like speaking to cattle; but Henrique with a frown told him that he was not obliged to wait his conveniency and time, adding that what was said was said, and was not again to be repeated, but do you or your people at your peril act contrary to our will. At that the other Indian was silent and durst not speak. These Mohooks are a terrour to all round them, and are certainly a brave, warlike people, but they are divided into two nations, Protestants and Roman Catholics, for the most of them are Christians; the first take part with the English, the latter with the French, which makes the neighbouring Indians, their tributaries, lead an unquiet life, always in fear and terrour and an uncertainty how to behave.

I went this night to visit Mr. Smibert, the limner, where I saw a collection of fine pictures, among the rest that part of Scipio's history in Spain where he delivers the lady to the prince to whom she had been betrothed. The passions are all well touched in the several faces. Scipio's face expresses a majestic generosity, that of the young prince gratitude and modest love; and some Roman soldiers, standing under a row of pillars apart, in seeming discourse, have admiration delineated in their faces. But what I admired most of the painter's fancy in this piece is an image or phantom of chastity behind the solium upon which Scipio sits, standing on tiptoe to crown him, and yet appears as if she could not reach his head, which expresses a good emblem of the virtue of this action. I saw here likewise a collection of good busts and statues, most of them antiques, done in clay and paste, among the rest Homer's head and a model of the Venus of Medicis.

Wednesday, July 25th. –I had appointed this day to go to Cambridge with Mr. Hooper, but the weather proved too hot. I went to Change at twelve o'clock, and heard no news, only some distant hints of an intended expedition of the English against Cape Briton, which is a great eyesore to their fishing trade upon this coast.

I dined with Mr. Hooper, and drank tea there, and went in the evening to the auction, but found no books of value exposed to sale. When I came to my lodging at night Mrs. Guneau told me she had got a new lodger, one Monsieur de la Moinnerie, a Frenchman, who had come from Jamaica. This evening was very hot, bordering upon our Maryland temperature, and being out of order 1 went to bed before nine.

Thursday, July 26th.–This day at Withered's I met with Dr. Clerk,' to whom I delivered a letter. He invited me to the Physical Club at the Sun Tavern' upon Friday evening. I promised to attend there in case the weather should prevent my journey eastward, which I intended as far as Portsmouth or Pitscataquay. I dined at Withered's with some gentlemen. While we were at dinner there came up a thunder shower, which cooled the air very much, it having been for some days very hot.

After dinner one Captain Pasher came in, who had been at Canso when the French took it. He had a vessel there laden with provisions, for which he had contracted with the French before the war broke out, when they carried him to Cape Breton. They were so generous as to pay him for his cargo of provisions and dismiss him. In the payment it was supposed they had given him some brandy and other contraband goods, which he attempted to run here, but being discovered was called to account by the government, not only for running these goods, but for supplying the enemy with provision. As to the latter accusation he was acquitted, because the contract or bargain with the French had been made before the declaration of war, and as he was taken prisoner at Canso, it was in the power of the French to seize his vessel and cargo without paying him for them. He had lost likewise considerably by his bills being protested by the Board of Admiralty in France. He told me his losses amounted to above 20,000 pounds New England currency. I imagined that he might be related to Mr. P–r at Annapolis, because I had known but few of that name. I asked him if he knew that gentleman. He replied that he had never seen him, but he believed he was a kinsman of his.

I went in the afternoon to Mr. Lechmere's, and thence to Mr. Fletcher's,2 a young gentleman, son to Captain Fletcher so well known in Annapolis. He and I went to the auction together, but the books sold so dear that I could not procure such as I wanted. We had only a good deal of auctioneer wit.

I supped at Fletcher's, and the night being very dark and rainy, I bad much ado to find my way home to my lodging, but calling in accidentally at Lechmere's without knowing where I went, he was so civil as to send a boy and lanthorn along with me. The streets of this town are very quiet and still a–nights, yet there is a constant watch kept in the town.

Friday, July 27th.–This day proving very rainy I was prevented in my intention to travel eastward. At breakfast with Mrs. Guneau, Mons. de la Moinnerie chattered like a magpie in his own language, having Mrs. Guneau to talk with, who speaks very good French. Their conversation ran upon the rate of the markets at Boston, and the price of beef, mutton, and other provisions. I dined at Withered's and in the afternoon went to the auction, where I bought a copy of Clerk's Homer very cheap. At night I went to the Physical Club at the Sun Tavern, according to appointment, where we drank punch, smoaked tobacco, and talked of sundry physical matters.

Douglass, the physician here, is a man of good learning, but mischievously given to criticism, and the most compleat snarler ever I knew. He is loath to allow learning, merit, or a character to anybody. He is of the clinical class of physicians, and laughs at all theory and practice founded upon it, looking upon empiricism or bare experience as the only firm basis upon which practice ought to be founded. He has got here about him a set of disciples, who greedily draw in his doctrines, and being but half learned themselves have not wit enough to discover the foibles and mistakes of their preceptor. This man I esteem a notorious physical heretic, capable to corrupt and vitiate the practice of the place by spreading his erroneous doctrines among his shallow brethren.

This night we heard news of Morpang's being upon the coast. I went home at eleven o'clock at night, and prepared for my journey to–morrow.

CHARLESTOWN FERRY

Saturday, July 28th. –I departed Boston this morning betwixt seven and eight o'clock, and crossing the upper ferry, I came to Charlestown, a pretty large and compact town, consisting of one street, about half a mile long.

I breakfasted there at the sign of the Swan. Our conversation at breakfast ran upon the extravagancies of the Newlightmen, and particularly one Gilman,' a noted preacher among them. One day this fellow being in his pulpit, he exerted himself to the utmost to move the passions in his audience by using such pathetic expressions as his dull, costive fancy could frame. "What!" said he, "not shed one tear for poor Christ, who shed his blood for you; not one tear, Christians! not one single tear! Tears for blood is but a poor recompense. *0 fie! fie!* this is but cold comfort." At that an old woman bolted up in pious fury, and mounting the pulpit steps, bestowed such a load of close hugs and kisses upon the preacher that she stopped his mouth for some time, and had almost suffocated him with kindness.

MYSTIC–LYNN

Departing Charlestown I passed thro' Mystic at ten o'clock, a pretty large village, about four miles northeast from Boston. A little after twelve I passed thro' Lynn, another village, but very scattered, and standing upon a large compass of ground, the situation very open and pleasant. Here I could have a view of the sea upon my right hand and upon my left, a large open hilly and rocky country with some skirts of woods which seemed to be but low and of a small growth.

MARBLEHEAD

At one o'clock I arrived at Marblehead, a large fishing town, lying upon the sea coast, built upon a rock, and standing pretty bleak to the easterly winds from the sea. It lies eighteen miles northeast from Boston, and is somewhat larger than Albany, but not so neatly or compactly built, the houses being all of wood and the streets very uneven, narrow, and irregular. It contains about 5,000 inhabitants and their commodity is fish. There is round the town above 200 acres of land covered with fish–flakes, upon which they dry their cod.

There are ninety fishing sloops always employed, and they deal for 134,000 sterling prime cost value in fish yearly, bringing in 30,000 quintals,–a quintal being one hundredweight dried fish, which is 3,000,000 pounds' weight, a great quantity of that commodity.

I put up here at one Reid's at the sign of the Dragon, and while I was at dinner, Mr. Malcolm,' the Church of England minister to whom I was recommended, came in. After I had dined he carried me round the town, and showed me the fishflakes and the town battery, which is built upon a rock, naturally well fortified, and mounts about twelve large guns. We had a great deal of talk about affairs at home. I went to his house and drank tea with him. He showed me some pretty pieces of music, and played some tunes on the flute and violin. He is author of a very good book upon music, which shows his judgment and knowledge in that part of science.

Sunday, July 29th.–This morning, inquiring for my portmanteau, I was told by my man Dromo that it was in his room. I had the curiosity to go and see what kind of a room his room was, and upon a reconnoitre found it a most spacious one, furnished *la mode de cabaret*, with tables, chairs, a fine feather–bed with quilted counterpane, white calico canopy or tester, and curtains, every way adapted for a gentleman of his degree and complexion.

I went to church to hear Mr. Malcolm in the forenoon, who gave us a pretty discourse. This church is a building of wood, about eighty feet square, supported in the inside with eight large octagonal wooden pillars of the Doric order. Upon this church stands a steeple in which there is a public clock. The floor of the church is raised six or seven feet above the ground, and under it is a burying place. The pulpit and altar are neat enough, the first being set out with a cushion of red velvet, and the other painted and adorned with the King's arms at top. There is one large gallery facing the pulpit, opposite to which at the south entry of the church hangs a pretty large gilt candle branch. The congregation consisted of about 400 people. I dined with Mr. Malcolm, and went to church again with him in the afternoon, and spent the in his company. In this town are likewise two great Presbyterian meetings.

SALEM

Monday, July 30th.–Mr. Malcolm and I set out at eleven o'clock in the morning for Salem, which is a pretty town about five miles from Marblehead, going round a creek, but not above two if you cross the creek. We arrived there betwixt twelve and one o'clock, and called at justice Sewell's, who invited us to dine with him. We put up our horses at the Ship Tavern,' and went to Mr. Sewell's.

Our conversation ran upon the enthusiasm now prevalent in these parts, and the strange madness that had possessed some people at Ipswitch, occasioned by one Woodberry,3 a mad enthusiast, who, pretending to inspiration, uttered several blasphemous and absurd speeches, asserting that he was the same to–day, yesterday, and forever, saying he had it in his power to save or damn whom he pleased, falling down upon the ground, licking the dust, and condemning all to hell who would not do the like, drinking healths to King Jesus, the selfexisting Being, and prosperity to the kingdom of heaven, and a thousand other such mad and ridiculous frolics. I was quite shocked at these relations, both when I heard them mentioned in conversation, and saw them published in the newspaper, being surprised that some of the chief clergy there had been so weak as to be drawn away by these follies. This is a remarkable instance to what lengths of madness enthusiasm will carry men once they give it a loose [rein], and tho' these excursions may appear shocking to people in their senses, yet so much good may follow them as that the interest and influence of these fanatic preachers will be thereby depressed among all such people as are not quite fools or mad. These extravagancies take all their first root from the labours of that righteous apostle Whitefield, who, only for the sake of private lucre and gain, sowed the first seeds of distraction in these unhappy ignorant parts.

In the afternoon Mr. Malcolm and I rid to the country–seat of one Brown,' a gentleman who married a daughter of the late Governour Burnet's, a grand–daughter of the bishop's. His house stands upon the top of a high hill, and is not yet quite finished. It is built in the form of an H, with a middle body and two wings. The porch is supported by pillars of the Ionic order about fifteen feet high, and betwixt the windows of the front are pilasters of the same. The great hall or parlour is about forty feet long and twenty–five wide, with a gallery over the first row of windows, and there are two large rooms upon a floor in each of the wings about twenty–five feet square.

From this hill you have a most extensive view. To the southwest you see the Blue Hills, about thirty–six miles' distance; to the east the sea and several islands; to the northwest the top of a mountain called Wachusett Mountain, like a cloud, about ninety miles' distance, towards Albany; and all round you have a fine landscape, covered with woods, a mixture of hills and valleys, land and water, upon which variety the eye dwells with pleasure. This hill Mr. Brown calls Mount Burnet in compliment to his wife.

In the hall I saw a piece of tapestry or arras of scripture history, done by Vanderbank, a Dutch artist. For elegance and design it is like painting, the passions in the faces being well expressed. It is the best of the kind ever I saw.

This gentleman has a fine estate, but withal has the character of being narrow and avaricious, a vice uncommon to young men. He has a strange taste for theological controversy. While we were there the conversation turned chiefly upon nice metaphysical distinctions relating to original sin, imputed righteousness, reprobation, effectual calling, and absolute decrees, which stuff–as I esteem it to be no more than the monstruous and deformed offspring of scholastic, theological heads, I should choose to hear at no other times but when I took a cathartic or emetic, in order to promote the operation if it proved too sluggish.

Mr. Malcolm and I returned to Salem a little before eight o'clock, and went to the Ship Tavern, where we drank punch and smoaked tobacco with several colonels; for colonels, captains, and majors are so plenty here that they are to be met with in all companies, and yet methinks they look no more like soldiers than they look like divines; but they are gentlemen of the place, and that is sufficient.

We went to Mr. Sewell's lodging betwixt nine and ten at night, and after some chat with him went to bed.

The town of Salem is a pretty place, being the first settled place in New England. In it there is one Church of England, one Quaker meeting, and five Presbyterian meetings. It consists of one very long street, running nearly east and west. Upon the watch–house, is a grenadier, carved in wood, shouldering his piece.

SALEM FERRY–IPSWITCH

Tuesday, July 31st.–At eleven o'clock this morning Mr. Malcolm accompanied me to Salem Ferry, where I crossed, and rid a pleasant level road all the way to Ipswitch, where the houses are so thick planted that it looks like one continued village. I put up at one Howel's in Ipswitch, at the sign of the Armed Knight. I waited upon Mr. John Rogers,1 the minister there, and delivered him a packet of letters from his son at Annapolis.

I returned again to the tavern and there met a talkative old fellow, who was very inquisitive about my place of abode and occupation, as he called it. He frequently accosted me with *please your honour*, with which grand title, like some fools whom I know, I seemed highly pleased tho I was conscious it did not belong to me. When I told him I came from Maryland, he said he had frequently read of that place but never had seen it. This old fellow, by his own account, had read of everything, but had seen nothing. He affected being a scholar, or a man much given to reading or study, and used a great many hard words in discourse, which he generally misapplied.

There was likewise a young man in company, who rid with me some miles on my way to Newberry. He valued himself much upon the goodness of his horse, and said that he was a prime beast as ever went upon four legs or wore hoofs. He told me he had a curiosity to ride to Maryland, but was afraid of the terrible woods in the way, and asked me if there were not a great many dangerous wild beasts in these woods. I told him that the most dangerous wild beasts in these woods were shaped exactly like men, and they went by the name of Buckskins, or Bucks, tho' they were not Bucks either, but something, as it were, betwixt a man and a beast. "Bless us! you don't say so," says he; "then surely you had needs ride with guns" (meaning my pistols). I parted with this wiseacre.

When I had got about half way to Newberry, a little farther I met a fat sheep driving in a chaise, a negro sitting upon the box. I asked the negro if that was his master. He told me no, but that it was a wether belonging to Mr. Jones, who had strayed and would not come home without being carried. Passing by this prodigy I met another, which was two great fat women riding upon one horse.

NEWBURY

I arrived at Newbury at seven o'clock, and put up at one Choat's at the sign of the Crown, which is a good house. Newbury is a pretty large village, lying close upon the water; the houses are chiefly wood. In this town there is one handsome meeting built in a square form, with a spire or steeple upon which is a little neat publick clock.

NEWBURY FERRY–HAMPTON

Wednesday, August 1st.–This morning proved very rainy, and therefore I did not set out till eleven o'clock. I crossed Newbury Ferry, and rid a pleasant even road, only somewhat stony, and in a perpetual drizzle, so that I could not have an advantageous view of the country round me. At half an hour after one I passed thro' Hampton, a very long, scattered town.

Having proceeded some miles farther, I was overtaken by a man who bore me company all the way to Portsmouth. He was very inquisitive about where I was going, whence I came, and who I was. His questions were all stated in the rustic civil style. "Pray, sir, if I may be so bold, where are you going?" "Prithee, friend," says I, "where are you going?" "Why, I go along the road here a little way." "So do I, friend," replied I. "But may I presume, sir, whence do you come?" "And from whence do you come, friend?" says I, "pardon me." "From John Singleton's farm," replied he, "with a bag of oats." "And I come from Maryland," said I, "with a portmanteau and baggage." "Maryland!" said my companion, "where the devil is that there place? I have never heard of it. But pray, sir, may I be so free as to ask your name?" "And may I be so bold as to ask yours, friend?" said 1. "Mine is Jerry Jacobs, at your service," replied he. I told him that mine was Bombast Huynhym van Helmont, at his service. "A strange name indeed; belike you 're a Dutchman, sir,–a captain of a ship, belike." "No, friend," says I, "I am a High German alchymist." "Bless us! you don't say so; that 's a trade I never heard of; what may you deal in, sir?" "I sell air," said I. "Air," said he, "damn it, a strange commodity. I 'd thank you for some wholesome air to cure my fevers, which have held me these two months." I have noted down this dialogue as a specimen of many of the same tenour I had in my journey when I met with these inquisitive rustics.

NEW HAMPSHIRE GOVERNMENT

Having now entered New Hampshire Government I stopped at a house within five miles of Portsmouth to bait my horses, where I had some billingsgate with a saucy fellow that made free in handling my pistols. I found a set of low rascally company in the house, and for that reason took no notice of what the fellow said to me, not being overfond of quarrelling with such trash. I therefore mounted horse again at half an hour after three, and having rid about two miles saw a steeple in a skirt of woods, which I imagined was Portsmouth; but when I came up to it, found it was a decayed wooden meeting house, standing in a small hamlet within two mile of Portsmouth.

PORTSMOUTH

In this part of the country one would think there were a great many towns by the number of steeples you see round you, every country meeting having one, which by reason of their slenderness and tapering form appear at a distance pretty high. I arrived in Portsmouth at four in the afternoon, which is a seaport town very pleasantly situated close upon the water, and nearly as large as Marblehead. It contains betwixt four and five thousand inhabitants. There are in it two Presbyterian meetings and one Church of England, of which last one Brown,' an Irishman, is minister, to whom I had a letter recommendatory from Mr. Malcolm. I put up here at Slater's, a widow woman, who keeps a very good house and convenient lodging. After I had dined, I waited upon Mr. Brown and he invited me to breakfast with him to–morrow. I returned to my lodging at eight o'clock, and the post being arrived, I found a numerous company at Slater's reading the news. Their chit–chat and noise kept me awake three hours after I went to bed.

Thursday, August 2d. –I went and breakfasted with Mr. Brown, and after breakfast we waited upon Governour Wentworth,' who received me very civily and invited me to take a souldier's dinner with him, as he called it, art the fort.

NEWCASTLE KITTERICK

At ten o'clock we went by water in the Governour's barge to Newcastle, a small town, two miles from Portsmouth, where the fort' stands upon a little island opposite to Newcastle. Upon the other side of the water, there is a village called Kitterick. The tide in these narrows runs with great rapidity and violence, and we having it in our favour and six oars in the barge, were down at the fort in about ten minutes. This fort is almost a triangle, standing on a rock facing the bay. That side next the town is about 200 feet long, built of stone, having a small bastion at each end. The other two sides next the water are each about 300 feet long, and consist of turf ramparts, erected upon a stone foundation, about seven feet high and ten feet thick, so that the largest bullets may lodge in it.

This fort mounts about thirty guns, most of them thirty–two pounders, besides fifteen or twenty small ones or twelve–pounders. In the guard–room, where we dined, are small arms for about sixty men, but kept in very bad order, being eat up with rust.

After dinner, the sky turning clear, we took a view to the eastward towards the ocean, and could see several islands and Cape Anne, at a distance like a cloud, with about twenty–four sail of small coasting vessels.

Mr. BROWN and I crossed the water at three o'clock, and rid nine miles up the country to a place called York. In our way we had a variety of agreeable prospects of a rocky and woody country and the ocean upon our right hand. We returned to the fort again a little after seven o'clock.

This Province of New Hampshire is very well peopled, and is a small colony or government, being enclosed on all hands by the Massachusetts Province, to which it once belonged, but has lately, for some state reasons, been made a separate government from New England.

The provinces here are divided into townships instead of shires or counties. The trade of this place is fish and masting for ships, the navy at home being supplied from here with very good masts.

I observed a good many geese in the fort. The Governour took notice that they were good to give an alarm in case of a nocturnal surprise, mentioning the known story of the Roman Capitol. We rowed back to town against the tide, betwixt eight and nine at night. I took my leave of Governour Wentworth at nine o'clock at night and went to my lodging.

HAMPTON

Friday, August 3d. –I departed Portsmouth at half an hour after five in the morning, and had a pleasant route to Hampton. This town is about seven or eight miles long, but so disjoined that some of the houses are half a mile's distance one from another. About the middle of it is a pretty large plain, about half a mile broad and four or five miles long, which is marshy and overgrown with saltwater hay. On my left hand here I could see the sea and Cape Anne, where the plain opened.

I breakfasted at one Griffin's at Hampton. I had some discourse with the landlord, who seemed to be very fond of speculative points of religion, and was for spiritualizing of everything.

NEWBURY FERRY

Near Newbury Ferry' I met an old man, who was very inquisitive about news. He rid above a mile with me. I crossed the ferry at twelve o'clock, and dined at Choat's with two Boston gentlemen, and after dinner they would have had me go to the Presbyterian meeting to hear a sermon, but I declined it, and getting upon horseback departed Newbury at three in the afternoon, the day being pretty hot.

Some miles from this town I passed thro' a pleasant small plain about a quarter of a mile broad, thro' the middle of which runs a pretty winding river. On the way I met a young sailor on foot who kept pace with my horse, and he told me he was bound for Salem that night. He entertained me with his adventures and voyages, and dealt much in the miraculous, according to the custom of most travellers and sailors.

IPSWITCH

I arrived at Ipswtch at six o'clock and put up at Howell's. I went to see Mr. Rogers, the minister there, and at night drank punch with his son, the doctor.

SALEM FERRY

Saturday, August 4th.–I left Ipswich early in the morning, and had a solitary ride to Salem. I put up my horses there at the Ship Tavern and called at Messrs. Sewell's and Brown's, but they were both gone out of town.

At Salem there is a fort' with two demi–bastions, but they stand less in need of it than any of the other maritime towns here, for the entry to this harbour is so difficult and rocky that even those who have been for years used to the place will not venture in without a good pilot, so that it would be a hard task for an enemy to enter. Portsmouth harbour is easy enough, but the current of the tides there is so violent that there is no getting in or out but at particular seasons, and, besides, they are locked in on all hands by islands and promontories. At Marblehead the entry is very easy and open.

At twelve o'clock I thought of going to Marblehead again to pay another visit to Mr. Malcolm, whose company and conversation had much pleased me, but meeting here with a gentleman going to Boston, I took the opportunity, for the sake of company, to i along with him.

LOWER FERRY

We rid hard to the lower ferry, having made fifteen miles in two hours. We had a tolerably good passage over the ferry, which here is two miles broad. I left my horses at Barker's stables, and drank tea with my landlady, Mrs. Guneau.

BOSTON

There was in the company a pretty young lady. The character of a certain Church of England clergyman in Boston was canvassed, he having lost his living for being too sweet upon his landlady's daughter, a great belly being the consequence. I pitied him only for his imprudence and want of policy. As for the crime, considered in a certain light, it is but a peccadillo, and he might have escaped unobserved, had he had the same cunning as some others of his brethren who doubtless are as deep in the dirt as he in the mire. I shall not mention the unfortunate man's name *(absit foeda calumnia)*, but I much commiserated his calamity and regretted the loss, for he was an excellent preacher; but the wisest men have been led into silly scrapes by the attractions of that vain sex.

I had the opportunity this night of seeing Mons. la Moinnerie, my fellow lodger. He was obliged to keep the house close, for fear of being made a prisoner of war. He was the strangest mortal for eating ever I knew. He would not eat with the family, but always in his own chamber, and he made a table of his trunk. He was always a–chewing, except some little intervals of time in which he applied to the study of the English language.

Sunday, August 5th.–I went this morning into monsieur's chamber and asked him how he did. He made answer in French, but asked me in maimed English if I had made *un bon voyage*, what news, and many other little questions culled out of his grammar. I was shy of letting him know I understood French, being loath to speak that language, as knowing my faultiness in the pronunciation. He told me that *hier au soir* he had de mos' excellen' *souper*, and wished I had been to eat along with him. His chamber was strangely set out: here a basin with the relicks of some soup, there a fragment of bread; here a paper of salt, there a bundle of garlic; here a spoon with some pepper in it, and upon a chair a saucer of butter. The same individual basin served him to eat his soup out of and to shave in, and in the water where a little before he had washed his hands and face, he washed likewise his cabbages. This, too, served him for a punchbowl. He was fond of giving directions how to dress his victuals, and told Nanny, the cook maid, "Ma foi, I be de good cock, Madame Nannie," said he. The maid put on an air of modest anger, and said she did not understand him. "Why, here you see," says he, "my cock be good, can dress *de fine viandes.*"

This morning I went and heard Mr. Hooper, and dined with Mr. Grey. I went to meeting again in the afternoon. He (Mr. Hooper) is one of the best preachers I have heard in America, his discourses being solid sense, strong connected reasoning, and good language. I drank tea with Mrs. Guneau in the afternoon, and staid at home this night, reading a little of Homer's first Iliad.

Monday, August 6th.–I was visited this morning by Mons. de la Moinnerie, who spoke bad English, and I indifferent French; so we had recourse to Latin, and did somewhat better. He gave me an account of his own country, their manners and government, and a detail of his own adventures since he came abroad. He told me that he had studied the law, and showed me a diploma granted him by the University of Paris. He had practised as a chamber counsel in Jamaica for two months, and was coming into pretty business, but intermeddling in some political matters procured the ill–will of the grandees there, and being obliged to go away, took to merchandizing; but his vessel being cast away at sea, he took passage for Boston in a sloop, before the French war was declared, intending to go from thence to old France.

I dined this day at Withered's, and spent the evening with Dr. Clerk, a gentleman of a fine natural genius, who, had his education been equivalent, would have outshone all the other physicians in Boston. Dr. D– was there and Mr. Lightfoot, and another gentleman, a lawyer, a professed connoisseur.

Dr. D– talked very slightingly of Boerhaave, and upon all occasions I find sets himself up as an enemy to his plan of theory, and laughs at all practice founded upon it. He called him a mere *helluo librorum*, an indefatigable compiler, that dealt more in books than in observation or [***].. I asked his pardon and told him that I thought he was by far the greatest genius that ever appeared in that way since the days of Hippocrates. He said his character was quite eclipsed in England. "Pardon me, sir," said I, "you are mistaken. Many of the English physicians who have studied and understand his system admire him. Such as have not, indeed, never understood him, and in England they have not as yet taught from his books; but till once they embrace his doctrines they will always, like the French, be lagging behind a century or two in the improvements of physick."

I could not learn his reasons for so vilifying this great man, and most of the physicians here (the young ones I mean) seem to be awkward imitators of him in this railing faculty. They are all mighty nice and mighty hard to please, and yet are mighty raw and uninstructed (excepting D– himself and Clerk) in even the very elements of physick. I must say it raised my spleen to hear the character of such a man as Boerhaave picked at by a parcel of pigmies, mere *homuncios* in physick, who shine nowhere but in the dark corner allotted them, like a lamp in a monk's cell, obscure and unknown to all the world excepting only their silly hearers and imitators, while the splendour of the great character which they pretend to canvass eclipses all their smaller lights like the sun enlightens all equally, is ever admired when looked upon, and is known by every one who has any regard for learning or truth. So that all their censure was like the fable of the dog barking at the moon. I found, however, that Dr. D– had been a disciple of Pitcairn's, and as some warm disputes had subsisted betwixt Pitcairn and Boerhaave, at his leaving the professional chair of Leyden, when turned out by the interest of King William (for Pitcairn was a strenuous Jacobite) he bore Boerhaave a mortal grudge afterwards, and endeavoured all he could to lessen his interest and diminish his character. I left the company at eleven o'clock and went home.

Tuesday, August 7th.–I was visited this morning by Monsieur.

I dined at Withered's and called at Mr. Hooper's after dinner to know when he intended to go for Cambridge; we agreed upon to–morrow afternoon. Coming home again I had the other volley of French from Monsieur, accompanied with a deal of action.

At night I went to the Scots' Quarterly Society, which met at the Sun Tavern. This is a charitable society, and act for the relief of the poor of their nation, having a considerable sum of money at interest, which they give out in small pensions to needy people. I contributed for that purpose three pounds, New England currency, and was presented with a copy of their laws.

When the bulk of the company were gone I sat some time with Dr. Douglass, the president, and two or three others, and had some chat on news and politicks. At half an hour after ten, I went home and had some more French from Monsieur, who was applying strenuously to learn English.

Wednesday, August 8th.–This proving a very rainy day, I was frustrated in my design of going to Cambridge, and was obliged to stay at home most of the day. I had several dialogues with La Moinnerie relating to the English language. Mr. Hughes and I eat some of his soup. By way of whet he made us some punch, and rinsing the bowl with water tossed it out upon the floor without any ceremony.

The French are generally the reverse of the Dutch in this respect. They care not how dirty their chambers and houses are, but affect neatness much in their dress when they appear abroad. I cannot say cleanliness, for they are dirty in their linen wear. Mr. Hughes and I dined with Mrs. Guneau, and went to Withered's. After dinner we walked out upon the Long Wharf.

The rain still continuing, I went home at four o'clock, and stayed at home all that evening.

Thursday, August 9th.–I went with Mr. Hughes before dinner to see my countrywoman Mrs. Blackater (here Blackadore, for our Scots names generally degenerate when transplanted to England, or English America, losing their proper orthography and pronunciation). She is a jolly woman, with a great round red face. I bought of her a pound of chocolate, and saw one of her daughters, a pretty buxom girl, in a gay tawdry deshabille, having on a robe de chambre of cherry–coloured silk, laced with silver round the sleeves and skirts, and neither hoop nor stays. By this girl's physiognomy, I judged she was one of that illustrious class of the sex commonly called coquettes. She seemed very handsome in every respect, and indeed needed neither stays nor hoop to set out her shapes, which were naturally elegant and good; but she had a vile cross in her eyes, which spoilt in some measure the beauty and symmetry of her features. Before we went away the old woman invited Hughes and me to drink tea any afternoon when at leisure.

I dined with Mr. Fletcher in the company of two Philadelphians, who could not be easy because forsooth they were in their nightcaps, seeing everybody else in full dress, with powdered wigs,–it not being customary in Boston to go to dine or appear upon Change in caps as they do in other parts of America. What strange creatures we are! and what trifles make us uneasy! It is no mean jest that such worthless things as caps and wigs should disturb our tranquillity and disorder our thoughts, when we imagine they are worn out of season. I was myself much in the same state of uneasiness with these Philadelphians, for I had got a great hole in the lappet of my coat, to hide which employed so much of my thoughts in company that, for want of attention I could not give a pertinent answer when I was spoke to.

I visited Mr. Smibert in the afternoon, and entertained myself an hour or two with his paintings. At night I was visited by Messrs. Parker and Laughton, who did not tarry long. Mr. Clerk came and spent the evening with me, and as we were a–discussing points of philosophy and physick our inquiries were interrupted by La Moinnerie, who entered the room with a dish of roasted mutton in his hand. "Messieurs, votre serviteur," says he. "Voil Voilà du mouton rôti ; voulez–vous manger un peu avec moi?" Dr. Clerk could not refrain laughing, but I payed a civil compliment or two to Monsieur and he retired, bowing, carrying his mutton with him.

I had occasion to see a particular diversion this day, which they call "hauling the fox."It is practised upon simple clowns. Near the town there is a pond of about half a quarter of a mile broad. Across this they lay a rope, and two or three strong fellows concealed in the bushes hold one end of it. To a stump in view there is tied a large fox. When they can lay hold of an ignorant clown, on the opposite side of the pond, they inveigle him by degrees into the scrape, two people pretending to wager,–one upon the fox's head, and the other upon the clown's,–twenty shillings or some such matter, that the fox shall not or shall pull him thro' the water in spite of his teeth. The clown easily imagines himself stronger than the fox, and for a small reward allows the rope to be put round his waist, which done, the sturdy fellows on the other side, behind the bush, pull lustily for their friend the fox, who sits tied to his stump all the time of the operation,–being only a mere spectator,–and haul poor pilgarlick with great rapidity thro' the pond, while the water hisses and foams on each side of him as he ploughs the surface, and his coat is well wet. I saw a poor country fellow treated in this manner. He ran thro' the water upon his back like a log of wood, making a frothy line across the pond, and when he came out he shook himself, and swore he could not have believed the fox had so much strength. They gave him twenty shillings to help to dry his coat. He was pleased with the reward, and said that for so much a time he would allow the fox to drag him thro' the pond as often as he pleased.

Friday, August 10th.–This morning proving very rainy, I could not go abroad till twelve o'clock. At that hour I went to Withered's, where I dined, and from thence walked down the Long Wharf with Mr. Hughes, Mr. Peach, and his brother.

We saw a French prize brought in, which was taken by Waterhouse, a Boston privateer. She was laden with wine, brandy, and some bail goods to the value of 14,000 sterling. They expected in two more (fishing vessels) taken by the same privateer. This Waterhouse has a well–fitted vessel and a great many stout hands, but by some misbehaviour in letting go a small privateer and a large merchant ship, he has acquired the character of cowardice. He was tried upon the affair before the Governour and Council, but acquitted himself tolerably, tho' his character must forever suffer by it.

We went on board of Mr. Peach's schooner, in the harbour, where we drank some Bristo' bottled cider. From thence we went to Close street, to visit Mrs. Blackater, where we saw the two young ladies, her daughters. They are both pretty ladies, gay and airy. They appear generally at home in a loose deshabille, which in a manner half hides and half displays their charms, notwithstanding which they are clean and neat. Their fine complexion and shapes are good, but they both squint and look two ways with their eyes. When they go abroad they dress in a theatrical manner, and seem to study the art of catching. There passed some flashes of wit and vivacity of expression in the conversation heightened no doubt by the influencing smiles of the young ladies. The old lady, after having under stood something of my history, gave me a kind invitation to come and practise physick in Boston, ani proffered me her business, and that of all the friend she could make, expressing a great regard for he countrymen and particularly for physicians of tha nation, who, she said, had the best character of any She entertained us much with the history of ; brother of hers, one Philips,' Governour of St. Mar tin's, a small Dutch settlement, and had got sever or eight copies of his picture done in graving, hunt up in her room. Peach passed her a compliment and said the pictures were exceeding like, for h knew her brother; but he told us afterwards tha they were only words of course, for there was n more likeness betwixt the man and his picture that betwixt a horse and a cow. This old woman i rich, and her daughters are reputed fortunes.

They are both beauties, and were it not for the squinting part they would be of the first rate.

After a very gay conversation of three hours, w –went away and I repaired to Withered's to the Physical Club, where Dr. D gave us a physical harangue upon a late book of surgery, published b., Heister,' in which he tore the poor author all b pieces and represented him as entirely ignorant o the affair. Heister is a man of such known learn ing and such an established character in Europe as sets him above any criticism from such a mal as D–, who is only a cynical mortal, so ful of his own learning that any other man's is not current with him. I have not as yet seen Heister's book of surgery, but D–'s criticism, instead of depreciating it in my opinion, adds rather to its character. I saw it recommended in the Physicw. *News* from Edinburgh, and the judgment of the *literati* in physick of that place preponderates with me all that D– can say against it. D– is of the clinical class of physicians, cries up empiricism, and practises upon grounds which neither he himself nor anybody for him can reduce to so much as a semblance of reason. He brags often of his having called Boerhaave a *helluo librorum* in a thesis which he published at Leyden, and takes care to inform us how much Boerhaave was nettled at it; just as much, I believe, as a mastiff is at the snarling of a little lapdog. There are in this town a set of half–learned physical prigs, to whom he is an oracle (Dr. Clerk only excepted, who thinks for himself). Leaving this company, quite sick of criticism I went home at eleven o'clock.

Saturday, August 11th.–I went this morning with Mr. Peach and breakfasted upon chocolate at the house of one Monsieur Bodineau, a Frenchman, living in School Street. This house was well furnished with women of all sorts and sizes. There were old and young, tall and short, fat and lean, ugly and pretty dames to be seen here. Among the rest was a girl of small stature,–no beauty, but there was life and sense in her conversation; her wit was mixed with judgment and solidity, her thoughts were quick, lively, and well expressed. She was, in fine, a proper mixture of the French mercury and English phlegm.

I went to Change at twelve o'clock, and dined with Mr. Arbuthnot. I had a tune on the spinet from his daughter after dinner, who is a pretty, agreeable lady, and sings well. I told her that she played the best spinet that I had heard since I came to America. The old man, who is a blunt, honest fellow, asked me if I could pay her no other compliment but that, which dashed me a little; but I soon replied that the young lady was every way so deserving and accomplished that nothing that was spoke in her commendation could in a strict sense be called a compliment. I breathed a little after this speech, there being something romantic in it, and considering human nature in a proper light, could not be true. The young lady blushed; the old man was pleased and picked his teeth; and I was conscious that I had talked nonsense.

I was disappointed in my intention of going to the Castle with Messieurs Parker and Laughton. They called before I came home, and left me, expecting that I would follow with Dr. Clerk, who did not keep the appointment. I rid out in the evening with Messrs. Peach and Hughes to one Jervise's, who keeps publick house four miles out of town. This house is the rendezvous of many of the gentry of both sexes, who make an evening's promenade in the summer time. There was a great deal of company, that came in chairs and on horseback. I saw there my old friend Captain Noise.' We drank punch, and returned to town at eight o'clock at night. After some comical chat with La Moinnerie, I went and supped at Withered's with Messrs. Peach and Hughes.

Sunday, August 12th.–I went this day, with Mr. Hughes and Peach, to Hooper's meeting, dined at Laughton's, and went again to meeting in the afternoon, where I saw Mrs. Blackater and her two daughters in a glaring dress.

This day I was taken notice of in passing the street by a lady who inquired of Mr. Hughes concerning me. "Lord!" said she, "what strange mortal is that?" "'T is the flower of the Maryland beaux," said Hughes. "Good God!" said the belle, "does that figure come from Maryland?" "Xtadam," said Hughes, "he is a Maryland physician." "O Jesus! a physician! deuce take such oddlooking physicians." I desired Hughes when he told me of this conference to give my humble service to the lady, and tell her that it gave me vast pleasure to think that anything particular about my person could so attract her resplendent eyes as to make her take notice of me in such a singular manner, and that I intended to wait upon her that she might entertain her opticks with my oddity, and I mine with her unparalleled charms.

I took a walk on the Long Wharf after sermon, and spent the evening very agreeably with Mr. Lightfoot and some other gentlemen at his lodging. Our discourse began upon philosophy, and concluded in a smutty strain.

Monday, August 13th. –I made a tour thro' the town in the forenoon with Mr. Hughes, and at a certain lady's house saw a white monkey. It was one of those that are brought from the Muscetto shore and seemed a very strange creature. It was about a foot long in its body, and in visage exceeding like an old man, there being no hair upon its face, except a little white downy beard. It laughed and grinned like any Christian (as people say), and was exceeding fond of its mistress, bussing her, and handling her bubbies just like an old rake. One might well envy the brute, for the lady was very handsome, so that it would have been no disagreeable thing for a man to have been in this monkey's place. It is strange to see how fond these brutes are of women, and, on the other hand, how much the female monkeys affect men. The progress of Nature is surprising in many such instances. She seems by one connected gradation to pass from one species of creatures to another, without any visible gap, interval, or *discontinuum* in her works. But an infinity of her operations is yet unknown to us.

I allotted this afternoon to go to the Castle with Messrs. Brazier and Hughes. Before dinner I called at Hooper's, and agreed to go to Cambridge with him to–morrow afternoon.

Brazier, Hughes, and I took horse after dinner, and rid round to the point, on purpose to go to the Castle, but were disappointed, no boat coming for us. It rained, and, as we returned home again, we called in at the Greyhound and drank some punch. Some children in the street took me for an Indian king upon account of my laced hat and sunburnt visage.

Tuesday, August 14th.–I went with La Moinnerie to dine at Withered's, he having now got a permission from the Governour to go abroad. We had there a good jolly company.

Mr. Hooper put off our going to Cambridge till to–morrow, so I went in the afternoon with Hughes to the house of Mr. Harding,' and had some conversation with a very agreeable lady there, Mr. Withered's sister. This lady cannot be deemed handsome, but to supply the want of that natural accomplishment, which the sex are so very fond of, she had a great deal of good sense and acquired knowledge, which appeared to the best advantage in every turn of her discourse. The conversation was lively, entertaining, and solid; neither tainted with false or trifling wit nor ill–natured satire or reflexion,–of late so much the topic of tea–tables. I was glad to find that in most of the politer cabals of ladies in this town, the odious theme of scandal and detraction over their tea had become quite unfashionable and unpolite, and was banished entirely to the assemblies of the meaner sort, where may it dwell forever, quite disregarded and forgotten, retiring to that obscure place Billingsgate, where the monster first took its origin.

Going from this house, we went and surveyed a ship upon the stocks, that was intended for a privateer. I spent the evening with Mr. Parker, where I drank good port wine, and heard news of six prizes carried into New York by the company of privateers there. There was in our company one Hill, who told us a long insipid story concerning a squint–eyed parson, a cat, and the devil. I had a letter from Miss Withered to her brother in Maryland, who lives upon Sassafras River.

Wednesday, August 15th.–I went this morning with Messrs. Hooper and Hughes to Cambridge. Upon the road we met two of the French Mohooks on horseback, dressed, *a la mode française*, with laced hats, full–trimmed coats, and ruffled shirts. One of them was an old fellow; the other a young man with a squaw mounted behind him. The squaw seemed to be a pretty woman, all bedaubed with wampum. They were upon little roan horses, and had a journey of above 700 miles to make by land. Upon the road to Cambridge, the lands are enclosed with fine stone fences, and some of the gates have posts of one entire stone, set right up upon end, about eight or ten feet high. The country all round is open and pleasant, and there is a great number of pretty country houses scattered up and down.

CAMBRIDGE

When we came to Cambridge we waited upon Mr. Hollyhoak,l the president, who sent the librarian 2 to show us the college and the library. Cambridge is a scattered town about the largeness of Annapolis, and is delightfully situated upon a pleasant plain near a pretty river of the same name,' over which is a wooden bridge. The college is a square building or quadrangle about 150 feet every way. The building upon the left hand as you enter the court is the largest and handsomest and most ancient, being about roo years old; but the middle or front building is indifferent, and of no taste. That upon the right hand has a little clock upon it, which has a very good bell. In the library are three or four thousand volumes with some curious editions of the classics, presented to the college by Dean Barklay. There are some curiosities, the best of which is the cut of a tree about ten inches thick and eight long, entirely petrified and turned into stone.

CHARLESTOWN FERRY–CASTLE OF BOSTON

We returned from Cambridge by the way of Charlestown. Crossing that ferry to Boston, we dined at Withered's with a pretty large company, and in the afternoon had a pleasant sail to the Castle, where the Governour and Assembly were met, to consult about fortifying of Governour's Island, which is situated just opposite to that whereon the Castle stands. This Castle consists of a large halfmoon with two bastions, defended with a glacis of earth and wood which is cannon proof. Upon these are mounted about forty great iron guns, each thirty–two–pounders. Upon the higher works or walls of this Castle are mounted above one hundred smaller guns, most of them twelve or eighteenpounders. Upon the most eminent place is a lookout, where stands the flag–staff, and where a sentry is always posted. From here you can see pretty plainly with a spy–glass.

LIGHTHOUSE

About nine miles farther out, upon a small island is the Lighthouse, which is a high stone building in form of a sugar–loaf, upon the top of which every night they burn oil, to direct and guide the vessels at sea into the harbour. There is a draw–well in the Castle, which is covered with an arch of brick and stone in fashion of a vault. In the most eminent place is a square court, upon one side of which is a chapel and stateroom, upon the other some dwelling–houses.

We went to see Mr. Philips, the chaplain there, and returned to town at nine o'clock at night. I supped with Hughes at Withered's, and saw one Mr. Simmonds there, a gentleman residing at Charleston in South Carolina, who was going there by land, and proposed to go in company with me to Maryland.

Thursday, August 26th.–I stayed at home most of the forenoon and had a deal of chat with La Moinnerie. I regretted much that I should be obliged to leave this facetious companion so soon, upon the account of losing his diverting conversation, and the opportunity of learning to speak good French, for he used to come to my room every morning and hold forth an hour before breakfast.

I intended to begin my journey homeward tomorrow. I dined with Hughes at Dr. Gardiner's, and our table talk was agreeable and instructing, divested of these trifles with which it is commonly loaded. We visited at Mrs. Blackater's in the afternoon, and had the pleasure of drinking tea with one of her fair daughters, the old woman and the other daughter being gone to their country farm.

I went in the evening with Mr. Hughes to a club at Withered's, where we had a deal of discourse in the disputatory way. One Mr. Clackenbridge (very properly so named upon account of the volubility of his tongue) was the chief disputant as to verbosity and noise, but not as to sense or argument. This was a little dapper fellow, full of the opinion of his own learning. He pretended to argue against all the company, but like a confused logician he could not hold an argument long, but wandered from one topic to another, leading us all into confusion and loud talking. He set up for a woman–hater, and preferring what he called liberty before every other enjoyment in life, he therefore decried marriage as a political institution, destructive of human liberty.

My head being quite turned this night with this confused dispute, and the thoughts of my journey to–morrow, I got into a strange fit of absence; for, having occasion to go out of the company two or three times to talk with Mr. Withered, I heedlessly every time went into a room where there was a strange company, as I returned, and twice sat down in the midst of them, nor did I discover I was in the wrong box till I found them all staring at me. For the first slip I was obliged to form the best apology I could, but at the second hit I was so confused and saw them so inclinable to laugh that I ran out at the door precipitately, without saying anything and betook me to the right company. I went to my lodging at twelve o'clock.

I need scarce take notice that Boston is the largest town in North America, being much about the same extent as the city of Glasgow in Scotland, and having much the same number of inhabitants, which is between twenty and thirty thousand. It is considerably larger than either Philadelphia or New York, but the streets are irregularly disposed, and in general too narrow. The best street in the town is that which runs down towards the Long Wharf, which goes by the name of King's Street. This town is a considerable place for shipping, and carries on a great trade in time of peace. There are now above one hundred ships in the harbour, besides a great number of small craft, tho' now upon account of the war the times are very dead. The people of this Province chiefly follow farming and merchandise. Their staples are shipping, lumber, and fish. The Government is so far democratic as that the election of the Governour's Council and the great officers is made by the members of the Lower House, or Representatives of the people. Mr. Shirley,' the present Governour, is a man of excellent sense and understanding, and is very well respected there. He understands how to humour the people, and at the same time acts for the interest of the Government.

Boston is better fortified against an enemy than any port in North America, not only upon account of the strength of the Castle, but the narrow passage up into the harbour, which is not above 16o feet wide in the channel at high water.

There are many different religions and persuasions here, but the chief sect is that of the Presbyterians. There are above twenty–five churches, chapels, and meetings in the town, but the Quakers here have but a small remnant, having been banished the Province at the first settlement upon account of some disturbances they raised. The people here have lately been, and indeed are now in great confusion and much infested with enthusiasm from the preaching of some fanatics and Newlight teachers, but now this humour begins to lessen. The people art generally more captivated with speculative than with practical religion. It is not by half such a flagrant sin to cheat and cozen one's neighbour, as it is to ride about for pleasure on the sabbath day, or to neglect going to church and singing of psalms. The middling sort of people here are to a degree disingenuous and dissembling, which appears even in their common conversation, in which their indirect and dubious answers to the plainest and fairest questions show their suspicions of one another. The better sort are polite, mannerly, and hospitable to strangers,–such strangers I mean as come not to trade among them (for of them they are jealous). There is more hospitality and frankness shown here to strangers than either at York or at Philadelphia, and in the place there is an abundance of men of learning and parts so that one is at no loss for agreeable conversation, nor for any set of company he pleases. Assemblies of the gayer sort are frequent here, the gentlemen and ladies meeting almost every week at concerts of musick and balls. I was present at two or three such, and saw as fine a ring of ladies, as good dancing, and heard musick as elegant as I had been wit ness to anywhere. I must take notice that this place abounds with pretty women, who appear rather more abroad than they do at York, and dress elegantly. hey are for the most part free and affable as well as pretty. saw not one prude while I was here.

The paper currency of these Provinces is now very much depreciated, and the price or value of silver rises every day, their money being now six for one upon sterling. They have a variety of paper currencies in the Provinces; viz., that of New Hampshire, the Massachusetts, Rhode Island, and Connecticut, all of different value, divided and subdivided into old and new tenors, so that it is a science to know the nature and value of their moneys, and what will cost a stranger some study and application.

Dr. Douglass has writ a compleat treatise upon all the different kinds of paper currencies in America,' which I was at the pains to read. It was the expense of the Canada expedition that first brought this Province in debt and put them upon the project of issuing bills of credit.

Their money is chiefly founded upon land security, but the reason of its falling so much in value is their issuing from time to time such large sums of it, and their taking no care to make payments at the expiration of the stated terms. They are notoriously guilty of this in Rhode Island Colony, so that now it is dangerous to pass their new moneys in the other parts of New England, it being a high penalty to be found so doing. This fraud must light heavily upon posterity. This is the only part ever I knew where gold and silver coin is not commonly current.

Friday, August 17th.– I left Boston this morning at half an hour after nine o'clock, and nothing I regretted so much as parting with La Moinnerie, the most lively and merry companion ever I had met with, always gay and chearful, now dancing and then singing, tho' every day in danger of being made a prisoner. This is the peculiar humour of the French in prosperity and adversity. Their temper is always alike, far different from the English, who, upon the least misfortune are for the most part clogged and overclouded with melancholy and vapours, and giving way to hard fortune shun all gayety and mirth. La Moinnerie was much concerned at my going away and wished me again and again *un bon voyage and bonne santé*, keeping fast hold of my stirrup for about a quarter of an hour.

DEDHAM

I had a solitary ride to Dedham, where I breakfasted at Fisher's and had some comical chat with Betty, the landlady's daughter, a jolly buxom girl. The country people here are full of salutations, even the country girls that are scarce old enough to walk will curtsy to one passing by. A great lubberly boy with short cut hair, having no cap, put his hand to his forehead as I passed him, in fashion as if he had been pulling off his cap.

WRENTHAM

I dined at Mann's in the town of Wrentham, at was served by a fat Irish girl, very pert and fo ward, but not very engaging. I proceeded the night to Hake's, where I lay. There was here large company, and among the rest a doctor, a to thin man, about whom nothing appeared remar: able but his dress. He had a weather–beaten black wig, an old striped collimancoe banyan and antique brass spur upon his right ankle, and pair of thick–soaled shoes tied with points. The told me he was the learnedest physician of the parts.

I went upstairs at nine o'clock and heard n landlady at prayers for an hour after I went to be The partition was thin, and I could distinctly he, what she said. She abounded with tautologies at groaned very much in the spirit, praying again at again for the fulness o f grace and the blessing 4 regeneration and the new birth.

Saturday, August 18th.–I set out from Hake's betwixt seven and eight in the morning, the weather being cloudy and close. I went by the way of Providence, which is a small but long town, situated close upon the water, upon rocky ground, much like Marblehead, but not a sixth part so large. It is the seat of Government in Providence Colony, there being an Assembly of the Delegates sometimes held here.

NANTUCKET FALL

About four miles northeast of this town there runs a small river, which falls down a rock, about three fathoms high, over which fall there is a wooden bridge. The noise of the fall so scared my horses that I was obliged to light and lead them over the bridge. At this place there are iron works. I breakfasted in Providence at one Angell's,2 at the sign of the White Horse, a queer pragmatical old fellow, pretending to great correctness of style in his common discourse. I found this fellow at the door, and asked him if the house was not kept by one Angell. He answered in a surly manner: "No." "Pardon me," says I, "they recommended me to such a house." So, as I turned away, being loath to lose his customer, he called me back. "Hark ye, friend," says he, in the same blunt manner, "Angell don't keep the house, but the house keeps Angell." I hesitated for some time if I should give this surly chap my custom, but resolved at last to reap some entertainment from the oddity of the fellow.

While I waited for the chocolate which I had ordered for breakfast, Angell gave me an account of his religion and opinions, which I found were as much out of the common road as the man himself. I observed a paper pasted upon the wall, which was a rabble of dull controversy betwixt two learned divines, of as great consequence to the publiek as *The Story o f the King and the Cobbler* or *The Celebrated History o f the Wise Men o f Gotharn*. This controversy was intituled *Cannons to batter the Tower of Babel*. Among the rest of the chamber furniture were several elegant pictures, finely illuminated and coloured, being the famous piece of *The Battle for the Breeches, The Twelve Golden Rules,* taken from King Charles I's study, of blessed memory (as he is very judiciously styled), *The Christian Coat o f Arms, & c., & c.,*, in which pieces are set forth divine attitudes and elegant passions, all sold by Overton, that inimitable ale–house designer at the White Horse without Newgate.

I left this town at ten o'clock, and was taken by some children in the street for a trooper, on account of my pistols.

PROVIDENCE FERRY–FERRY BRISTO'–FERRY RHODE ISLAND

I crossed Providence Ferry betwixt ten and eleven o'clock, and after some difficulty in finding my way, I crossed another ferry about four miles eastward of Bristol. I arrived in Bristol at one o'clock, and a little after crossed the ferry to Rhode Island, and dined at Burden's. I departed thence at four o'clock, but was obliged to stop twice before I got to Newport upon the account of rain.

I went into a house for shelter, where were several young girls, the daughters of the good woman of the house. They were as simple and awkward as sheep, and so wild that they would not appear in open view, but kept peeping at me from behind doors, chests, and benches. The country people in this island in general are very unpolished and rude.

I entered Newport betwixt seven and eight at night, a thick fog having risen, so that I could scarce find the town. When within a quarter of a mile of it my man, upon account of the portmanteau, was in the dark taken for a peddler by some people in the street, whom I heard coming about him and inquiring what he had got to sell. I put up at Niccoll's, at the sign of the White Horse, and lying there that night was almost eat up alive with bugs.

Sunday, August 19th.–I called upon Dr. Moffatt in the morning, and went with him to a windmill near the town to look out for vessels, but could spy none. The mill was a–going, and the miller in it grinding of corn, which is an instance of their not being so observant of Sunday here as in the other parts of New England.

I dined at Dr. Moffatt's lodging, and in the afternoon went to a Baptist meeting to hear sermon. A middle–aged man preached, and gave us a pretty good tho' trite discourse upon morality. I took lodging at one Mrs. Leech's, a Quaker, who keeps an apothecary's shop, a sensible, discreet, and industrious old woman.

Dr. Moffatt took me out this evening to walk near the town, where are a great many pleasant walks amidst avenues of trees. We viewed Mr. Malbone's house and gardens, and as we returned home met Malbone himself, with whom we had some talk about news. We were met by a hand some bona–roba in a flaunting dress, who laughed us full in the face. Malbone and I supposed she was a paramour of Moffatt's, for none of us knew her. We bantered him upon it, and discovered the truth of our conjecture by raising a blush in his face.

Monday, August 20th.–I made a tour round the town this morning with Dr. Moffatt. I dined with him, and in the afternoon went to the coffee–house, and after drinking a dish of coffee, we went with Mr. Grant, a Scotch gentleman in town, and took a walk across one end of the island, where we had several delightful views to the water. There is one cliff here, just bluff upon the ocean, called Hog's–hole, out of which filtre some springs of very fine fresh water. It affords a cool, pleasant shade in the summer time, for which reason the ladies go there to drink tea in a summer's afternoon. We encountered some fair dames there, and had abundance of gallantry and romping.

At seven o'clock I went with one Mr. Scot' to a Club, which sits once a week upon Mondays, called the Philosophical Club. But I was surprised to find that no matters of philosophy were brought upon the carpet. They talked of privateering and building of vessels; then we had the history of some old families in Scotland, where, by the bye, Grant told us a comic piece of history relating to General Wade' and Lord Lovat. The latter had somehow fore made it his business to get him turned out of a Colonel's commission which he then possessed. What he accused him of was his keeping a ragamuffin company of cowherds and other such trash to make the number of his regiment compleat, while he put the pay in his own pocket. Wade upon a time comes to review this regiment. Lovat being advertised beforehand of this review laid his scheme so that he procured a parcel of likely fellows to come upon the field, who made a tolerable appearance. When the General had reviewed them, my Lord asked him what he thought of his men. "Very good cowherds in faith, my Lord," replied the General. Lovat asked what his Excellency meant by that reply. The General answered that he was ordered to signify his Majesty's pleasure to him that he should serve no longer as Colonel of that regiment. "Look ye, sir," says Lovat, "his Majesty may do in that affair as he pleases; it is his gift, and he may take it again, but one thing he cannot without just reason take from me, which makes a wide difference betwixt you and me." Wade desired him to explain himself. "Why, thus it is," says Lovat : "When the king takes away my commission I am still Lord Lovat; when he takes yours away, pray observe, sir, that your name is George Wade." This unconcerned behaviour nettled Wade very much and blunted the edge of his revenge. After this history was given, the company fell upon the disputes and controversies of the fanatics of these parts, their declarations, recantations, letters, advices, remonstrances, and other such damned stuff, of so little consequence to the benefit of mankind or the publick that I looked upon all time spent ii either talking concerning them or reading thei works as eternally lost and thrown away, and there fore disgusted with such a stupid subject of dis course, I left this Club and went home.

Tuesday, August 21st.–I stayed at home most of the forenoon and read Murcius, which I had of Dr. Moffatt, a most luscious piece, from whom all our modern salacious poets have borrowed their thoughts. I did not read this book upon account of its lickerish contents, but only because I knew it to be a piece of excellent good Latin, and I wanted to inform myself of the proper idiom of ye language upon that subject.

I walked out betwixt twelve and one with Dr. Moffatt, and viewed Malbone's house and gardens. We went to the lanthern or cupola at top, from which we had a pretty view of the town of Newport and of the sea towards Block Island, and behind the house of a pleasant mount, gradually ascending to a great height, from which we can have a view of almost the whole island. Returning from thence, we went to the coffee–house, where, after drinking some punch, the doctor and I went to dine with Mr. Grant. After dinner I rid out of town in a chaise with Dr. Keith, one Captain Williams' accompanying us on horseback.

WHITEIIALL

We called at a publick house, which goes by the name of Whitehall, kept by one Anthony, about three miles out of town, once the dwelling–house of the famous Dean Barclay,' when in this island, and built by him. As we went along the road, we had a number of agreeable prospects.

At Anthony's we drank punch and tea, and had the company of a handsome girl, his daughter, to whom Captain Williams expressed a deal of gallantry. She was the most unaffected and best behaved country girl ever I met with. Her modesty had nothing of the prude in it, nor had her frolicksome freeness any dash of impudence.

We returned to town at seven o'clock, and spent the rest of the night at the coffee–house, where our ears were not only frequently regaled with the sound of *very welcome, sir,* and *very welcome, gentlemen,* pronounced solemnly, slowly, and with an audible voice to such as came in and went out by Hassey, a queer old dog, the keeper of the coffeehouse, but we were likewise alarmed (not charmed) for half an hour by a man who sang with such a trumpet note that I was afraid he would shake down the walls of the house about us. I went home betwixt nine and ten o'clock.

Wednesday, August 22d.–I stayed at home all this morning, and betwixt twelve and one, going to the coffee–house, I met Dr. Keith and Captain Williams. We tossed the news about for some time. Hassey, who keeps this coffee–house, is a comical old whimsical fellow. He imagines that he can discover the longitude, and affirms that it is no way to be done but by an instrument made of whalebone and cartilage or gristle. He carried his notions so far as to send proposals to the Provincial Assembly about it, who, having called him before them, he was asked if he was a proficient in the mathematicks. "Why, lookee, gentlemen," says he, "suppose a great stone lies in the street, and you want to move it, unless there be some moving cause, how the devil shall it move?" The Assembly finding him talk thus in parables, dismissed him as a crazy gentleman, whom too little learning had made mad. He gives this as his opinion of Sir Isaac Newton and Lord Verulam, that they were both very great men, but still they both had certain foibles, by which they made it known that they were mortal men, whereas had he been blessed with such a genius, he would have made the world believe that he was immortal, as both Enos and Elias had done long ago. He talks much of cutting the American isthmus in two, so to make a short passage to the south seas, and if the powers of Europe cannot agree about it he says he knows how to make a machine with little expense, by the help of which ships may be dragged over that narrow neck of land with all the ease imaginable, it being but a trifle of loo miles, and so we may go to the East Indies, a much easier and shorter way than doubling the Cape of Good Hope. He has a familiar phrase, which is, "very welcome, sir," and "very welcome, gentlemen," which he pronounces with a solemn sound, as often as people come in or go out.

I dined with Captain Williams and at six o'clock went again to the coffee–house. At seven we called upon some ladies in town, and made an appointment for a promenade. In the meantime Dr. Keith and I went to the prison, and there had some conversation with a French gentleman, a prisoner, and with one judge Pemberton,' a man of good learning and sense. While we were there one Captain B;,112 called in, who seemed to be a droll old man. He entertained us for half an hour with comical stories and dry jokes. At eight o'clock we waited on the ladies, and with them walked a little way out of town to a place called the Little Rock. Our promenade continued two hours, and they entertained us with several songs. We enjoyed all the pleasures of gallantry without transgressing the rules of modesty or good manners. There were six in company at this promenade; viz., three dames and three gallants. The belle who fell to my lot pleased me exceedingly, both in looks and conversation. Her name was Miss Clerk,' daughter to a merchant in town. After a parting salute, according to the mode of the place, I with reluctance bid the ladies farewell, expressing some regret that being a stranger in their town, and obliged soon to leave it, I should perhaps never have the happy opportunity of their agreeable company again. They returned their good wishes for my compliment, so I went to my lodging, and, after some learned chat with my landlady concerning the apothecary's craft, I went to bed.

Thursday, August 23d.–It rained hard all this morning, and therefore I stayed at home till twelve o'clock. Mr. Moffatt came to breakfast with me, and he and I went to the coffee–house betwixt twelve and one. We saw there some Spaniards that had been taken in the snow prize. One of them was a very handsome man and well behaved; none of that stiffness and solemnity about him commonly ascribed to their nation, but perfectly free and easy in his behaviour, rather bordering upon the French vivacity. His name was Don Manuel (I don't know what). He spoke good French and Latin, and ran out very much in praise of the place, the civility and humanity of the people, and the charms of the ladies.

I dined at Mr. Grant's, and went with Dr. Moffatt in the afternoon to visit Dr. Brett, where we had a deal of learned discourse about microscopical experiments, and the order, elegance, and uniformity of Nature in the texture of all bodies, both animate and inanimate. I spent the evening at Dr. Moffatt's lodging, along with Mr. Wanthon,l the collector, and Mr. Grant, a young gentleman of the place, and Dr. Brett, and returned to my lodging at ten o'clock.

I found the people in Newport very civil and courteous in their way. I had several invitations to houses in town, all of which because of my short stay I could not accept of. They carry on a good trade in this place in time of peace, and build a great many vessels. The island is famous for making of good cheeses, but I think those made in the Jerseys as good, if not preferable. In time of war this place is noted for privateering, which business they carry on with great vigour and alacrity. The island has fitted out now thirteen or fourteen privateers, and is daily equipping more.

While I stayed in this place they sent in several valuable prizes, but, notwithstanding this warlike apparatus abroad, they are but very sorrily fortified at home. The rocks in their harbour are the best security; for the fort, which stands upon an island, about a mile from the town, is the futilest thing of that nature ever I saw. It is a building of near aoo feet square, of stone and brick, the wall being about fifteen feet high, with a bastion and watch–tower on each corner, but so exposed to cannon shot that it could be battered about their ears in ten minutes. A little distance from this fort is a battery of seventeen or eighteen great guns.

They are not so strait–laced in religion here as in the other parts of New England. They have among them a great number of Quakers. The island is the most delightful spot of ground I have seen in America. I can. compare it to nothing but one entire garden. For rural scenes and pretty, frank girls, I found it the most agreeable place I had been in thro' all my peregrinations.

I am sorry to say that the people in their dealings one with another, and even with strangers in matters of truck or bargain, have as bad a character for chicane and disingenuity as any of our American Colonies. Their government is somewhat democratick, the people choosing their Governour from among their own number every year by poll votes.

One Mr. Green' is now Governour; the House of Assembly chooses the Council. They have but little regard to the laws of England, their mother country, tho' they pretend to take that constitution for a precedent.

Collectors and naval officers here are a kind of ciphers. They dare not exercise their office for fear of the fury and unruliness of the people, but their places are profitable, upon account of the presents they receive for every cargo of run goods. This Colony separated itself from New England, and was formed into a different government thro' some religious quarrel that happened betwixt them. It is customary here to adorn their chimney panels with birds' wings, peacock feathers, and butterflies.

Friday, August 24th.–Going to breakfast this morning I found a stranger with Mrs. Leech, who in sixteen days had come from Maryland, and had been there about some business relating to iron works. When I came into the room he asked Mrs. Leech if this was the gentleman that came from Maryland. She replied yes; then turning to me he acquainted me that he had lately been there, and had seen several people whom he supposed I knew, but he was fain to leave the place in a hurry, the agues and fevers beginning to be very frequent. He gave me an account of his having seen some of my acquaintances well at Joppa. I was glad to hear good news from home, it being now above three months since I had any intelligence from there.

I called at Dr. Moffatt's after breakfast, who entertained me for half an hour with his sun microscope, which is a very curious apparatus, and not only magnifies the object incredibly, upon the movable screen, but affords a beautiful variety and surprising intermixture of coloars. He showed me a small spider, the down of a moth's wing, the down of feathers, and a fly's eye, in all of which objecis Nature's uniformity and beautiful design, in the most minute parts of her work, appeared. The doctor walked to the ferry landing with me, and there we took leave of one another. 515.

CONNANICUT FERRY–NARRAGANSETT FERRYKINGSTOWN

I had a tedious passage to Connanicut. It being quite calm we were obliged to row most of the way. Our passage was more expeditious over Narragansett Ferry, and there I had the company of a Rhode Islander all the way to Kingstown, where I dined at Case's in the company of some majors and captains, it being a training day. Betwixt Case's and Hill's I was overtaken by a gentleman of consider able fortune here. He has a large house close upon the road, and is possessor of a very large farm, where he milks daily 104 cows, and has besides a vast stock of other cattle. He invited me into his house, but I thanked him and proceeded, the sun being low.

I put up at Hill's about sunset, and inquired there at the landlord concerning this gentleman. Hill informed me that he was a man of great estate, but of base character, for being constituted one of the committee for signing the public bills of credit, he had counterfeited 50,000 pounds of false bills, and made his brethren of the committee sign them, and then counterfeited their names to 50,000 pounds of genuine bills, which the government had then issued.

This piece of villany being detected the whole Ioo,ooo pounds was called in by the Government and he fined in 30,000 pounds to save his ears. But I think the fate of such a wealthy villain should have been the gallows, and his whole estate should have gone to repair the publick damage.

As one rides along the road in this part of the country, there are whole hedges of barberries.

Saturday, August 25th.–I set off at seven o'clock from Hill's, and it being a thick mist I had a dull solitary ride to Thomson's, where I breakfasted, being overtaken by a Seventh–day man going to meeting. Thankful, a jolly, buxom girl, the landlady's daughter, made me some chocolate, for which I did not thank her, it being sorry stuff. I departed from there a little after ten, in the company of some Seventh–day men going to meeting.

CONNECTICUT GOVERNMENT– STONINGTON

In this government of Rhode Island and Providence, you may travel without molestation upon Sunday, which you cannot do in Connecticut or the Massachusetts Province without a pass, because here they are not agreed what day of the week the sabbath is to be kept, some observing it upon Saturday and others upon Sunday.

I dined at Williams's at Stonington with a Boston merchant named Gardiner, and one Boyd, a Scotch Irish peddler. The peddler seemed to understand his business to a hair. He sold some dear bargains to Mrs. Williams, and while he smoothed her up with palaver the Bostoner amused her with religious cant. This peddler told me he had been some time ago at Annapolis, at some horse races, and inquired after some people there. He gave me a description of B– ie M–t, whose lodger he had been, and gave me a piece of secret history concerning P–l R–z, the Portuguese, and N–y H–y, how they passed for man and wife when they were in Philadelphia and the neighbourhood of that city. Our conversation at dinner was a medley. Gardiner affected much learning and the peddler talked of trade.

NEW LONDON FERRY–NEW LONDON

I left Williams's about half an hour after three, and icrossing the ferry a little after five o'clock, I arrived at New London and put up at Duchand's, at the sign of the Anchor. I did not know till now that I had any relations in this town. A parcel of children, as I rid up the lane, saluted me with "How d'ye, uncle? Welcome to town, uncle."

Sunday, August 26th.–I stayed at home most of the forenoon, and was invited to dine with Collector Lechmere, son to the surveyor at Boston. There was at table there one Dr. Goddard and an old maid, whom they called Miss Katy, being a great fat woman with a red face, as much like an old maid as a frying–pan. There sat by her a young modestlooking lady, dressed in black, whom Mr. Lechmere called Miss Nancy, and next her, a walnut–coloured thin woman, sluttishly dressed, and very hard favoured.

These ladies went to meeting after dinner, and we three sat drinking of punch, and telling of droll stories.

I went home at six o'clock, and Deacon Green's son came to see me. He entertained me with the history of the behaviour of one Davenport,' a fanatick preacher there, who told his flock in one of his enthusiastic rhapsodies, that in order to be saved they ought to burn all their idols. They began this conflagration with a pile of books in the publick street, among which were Tillotson's *Sermon*, Beveridge's *Thoughts*, Drillincourt on *Death*, Sherlock, and many other excellent authors, and sang psalms and hymns over the pile while it was a–burning. They did not stop here, but the women made up a lofty pile of hoop petticoats, silk gowns, short cloaks, cambrick caps, red–heeled shoes, fans, necklaces, gloves, and other such apparel, and, what was merry enough, Davenport's own idol, with which he topped the pile, was a pair of old wore–out plush breeches, but this bonfire was happily prevented by one more moderate than the rest, who found means to persuade them that making such a sacrifice was not necessary for their salvation, and so every one carried off their idols again, which was lucky for Davenport . . ., for the devil another pair of breeches had he but these same old plush ones which were going to be offered up as an expiatory sacrifice. Mr. Green took his leave of me at ten o'clock, and I went to bed.

Monday, Augusta7th.–Aftervisiting Deacon Green this morning, and drinking tea with him and wife, he gave me a packet for his son Jonas at Annapolis. The old man was very inquisitive about the state of religion with us, what kind of ministers we had, and if the people were much addicted to godliness. I told him that the ministers minded hogsheads of tobacco more than points of doctrine, either orthodox or heterodox, and that the people were very prone to a certain religion called *self–interest*.

HANTICK FERRY

I left New London betwixt eight and nine o'clock in the morning, and crossed Hantick Ferry' or the Gut, a little before ten. This is an odd kind of a ferry, the passage across it not being above fifty paces wide, and yet the inlet of water here from the Sound is near three–quarters of a mile broad. This is occasioned by a long narrow point or promontory of hard sand and rock, at its broadest part not above twelve paces over, which runs out from the western towards the eastern shore of this inlet, and is above half a mile long, so leaves but a small gut, where the tide runs very rapid and fierce. The scow that crosses here goes by a rope, which is fixed to a stake at each side of the gut, and the scow is fastened to the main rope by an iron ring, which slides upon it, else the rapidity of the tide would carry scow and passengers and all away.

NANTIQUE, AN INDIAN TOWN

A little after I passed this ferry I rid close by an Indian town upon the left hand situated upon the brow of a hill. This town is called Nantique and consists of thirteen or fourteen huts or wigwams made of bark.

TOLL-BRIDGE-CONNECTICUT RIVER

I passed over a bridge in very bad repair, for which I paid eightpence toll, which here is something more than a penny farthing sterling, and coming down to Seabrook Ferry upon Connecticut River, I waited there three or four hours, at the house of one Mather, before I could get passage. The wind blew hard at northwest with an ebb tide, which the ferrymen told me would have carried us out into the Sound had we attempted to pass.

Mather and I had some talk about the opinions lately broached here in religion. He seemed a man of some solidity and sense, and condemned Whitefield's conduct in these parts very much. After dinner there came in a rabble of clowns, who fell to disputing upon points of divinity as learnedly as if they had been professed theologues. 'T is strange to see how this humour prevails, even among the lower class of the people here. They will talk so pointedly about justification, sanctification, adoption, regeneration, repentance, free grace, reprobation, original sin, and a thousand other such pretty chimerical knickknacks, as if they had done nothing but studied divinity all their lifetime, and perused all the lumber of the scholastic divines, and yet the fellows look as much, or rather more like clowns, than the very riffraff of our Maryl2nd planters. To talk in this dialect in our parts would be like Greek, Hebrew, or Arabick.

I met with an old paralytic man in this house, named Henderson, who let me know that he had travelled the world in his youthful days and had been in Scotland, and lived some years in Edinburgh. He condemned much the conduct of the late enthusiasts here, by which he put some of our clowns in company in a fret, but the old man regarded them not, going on with his discourse, smoking his pipe, and shaking his gray locks. I was very much taken with his conversation, and he seemingly with mine, for he gave me many a hearty shake by the hand at parting, and wished me much prosperity, health, and a safe return home.

SEABROOK FERRY–SEABROOK

I crossed the ferry at five o'clock. This river of Connecticut is navigable for fifty miles up the country. Upon it are a good many large trading towns, but the branches of the river run up above two hundred miles. We could see the town of Seabrook below us on the western side of the river.

I lodged this night at one Mrs. Lay's, a widow woman, who keeps a good house upon the road, about six miles from Seabrook. I had much difficulty to find the roads upon this side Connecticut River. They wind and turn so much, and are divided into such a number of small paths. I find they are not quite so scrupulous about bestowing titles here as in Maryland. My landlady goes here by the name of Madam Lay. I cannot tell for what, for she is the homeliest piece both as to mien, make, and dress that ever I saw, being a little round–shouldered woman, pale–faced and wrinkly, clothed in the coarsest homespun cloth; but it is needless to dispute her right to the title, since we know many upon whom it is bestowed who have as little right as she.

Tuesday, August 28th.–I departed Lay's at seven in the morning, and rid some miles thro' a rocky high land, the wind blowing pretty sharp and cool at northwest.

KILLINGSWORTH

A little after eight o'clock, I passed thro' Killingsworth, a small town, pleasantly situated. I breakfasted at one Scran's, about half way betwixt Killingsworth and Gilford. This is a jolly old man, very fat and pursy, and very talkative and full of history. He had been an American soldier in Queen Anne's war, and had travelled thro' most of the continent of North America.

He inquired of me if poor Dick of Noye was alive, which question I had frequently put to me in my travels.

GILFORD

Going from this house, I passed thro' Gilford at eleven o'clock in company of an old man, whom I overtook upon the road. He showed me a curious stone bridge, within a quarter of a mile of this town. It lay over a small brook, and was one entire stone about ten feet long, six broad, and eight or ten inches thick, being naturally bent in the form of an arch, without the help of a chisel to cut it into that shape. "Observe here, sir," says the old man, "you may ride i,ooo miles and not meet with such a stone." Gilford is a pretty town, built upon a pleasant plain. In it there is a meeting, upon the steeple of which is a publiek clock.

ZANFORD

I came to Branford, another scattered town, built upon high rocky ground, a little after one o'clock, where I dined at the house of one Frazer. Going from thence I passed thro' a pleasant, delightful part of the country, being a medley of fine green plains, and little rocky and woody hills, caped over as it were with bushes.

VEWHAVEN FERRY–NEWHAVEN

I crossed Newhaven Ferry betwixt four and five o'clock in the afternoon. This is a pleasant navigable river that runs thro' a spacious green plain into the Sound. 539.

I arrived in Newhaven at five o'clock, where I put up at one Monson's at ye sign of ye Half–moon. There is but little good liquor to be had in the publick houses upon this road. A man's horses are better provided for than himself, but he pays dear for it. The publick–house keepers seem to be somewhat wild and shy when a stranger calls. It is with difficulty you can get them to speak to you, show you a room, or ask you what you would have, but they will gape and stare when you speak, as if they were quite astonished. Newhaven is a pretty large, scattered town, laid out in squares, much in the same manner as Philadelphia, but the houses are sparse and thin sown. It stands on a large plain, and upon all sides (excepting the south, which faces the Sound) it is enclosed with ranges of little hills, as old Jerusalem was, according to the topographical descriptions of that city. The buryingplace is in the center of the town, just facing the college,' which is a wooden building about Zoo feet long, and three stories high, in the middle front of which is a little cupola, with a clock upon it. It is not so good a building as that at Cambridge, nor are there such a number of students. It was the gift of a private gentleman to this place.

MILLFORD

Wednesday, August 29th.–I set out from Monson's a little after seven o'clock, and rid a tolerable good road to Millford. Before I came there I was overtaken by a young man, who asked me several questions, according to country custom,– such as where I was going and whence I came, and the like. To all which I gave answers just as impertinent as the questions were themselves. I breakfasted in Millford at one Gibbs's, and while I was there, the post arrived, so that there came great crowds of the politicians of the town to read the news, and we had plenty of orthographical blunders. We heard of some prizes taken by the Philadelphia privateers. Millford is a large scattered town, situated upon a large pleasant plain.

STRATFORD FERRY- STRATFORD

I went from here in company of a young man, and crossed Stratford Ferry at eleven o'clock, and was obliged to call at Stratford, my gray horse having lost a shoe. I stayed there some time at one Benjamin's, who keeps a tavern in the town. There I met a deal of company, and had many questions asked me. Stratford is a pleasant little town, prettily situated upon a rising ground, within half a mile of a navigable river that runs into the Sound. In this town is one Presbyterian meeting, and one church, both new buildings. The church is built with some taste and elegance, having large arched sash windows, and a handsome spire or steeple at the west end of it.

FAIRFIELD

My young man rid with me till I came within five miles of Fairfield, which is another town in which is an octagonal church or meeting built of wood, like that of Jamaica upon Long Island, upon the cupola of which is a publick clock.

The roads between this town and Norwalk are exceeding rough and stony, and the stones are very full of glittering isinglass.

There is a river on the west side of this town, which runs into the Sound. I forded it at high water, when pretty deep.

SAGATICK RIVER

Within three miles and a half of Norwalk is another river, called by the Indian name of Sagatick. This I forded at low tide. I dined at one Taylor's here. My landlord was an old man of seventy. Understanding from my boy that I was a doctor from Maryland, and having heard that some of the doctors there were wonder–workers in practice, he asked my advice about a cancer which he had in his lip. I told him there was one Bouchelle in Maryland who pretended to cure every disease by the help of a certain water which he had made, but as for my part I knew no way of curing a cancer but by extirpation or cutting it out.

NORWALK

I arrived at Norwalk at seven o'clock at night. This town is situated in a bottom, midst a grove of trees. You see the steeple shoot up among the trees about half a mile before you enter the town and before you can see any of the houses.

While I was at Taylor's the children were frightened at my negro. Slaves are not so much in use as with us, their servants being chiefly bound or indentured Indians. The child asked if that negro was a–coming to eat them up. Dromo indeed wore a voracious phiz, for, having rid twenty miles without eating, he grinned like a crocodile, and showed his teeth most hideously.

Betwixt Taylor's and Norwalk, I met a caravan of eighteen or twenty Indians. I put up at Norwalk at one Beelding's, and as my boy was taking off the saddles, I could see one half of the town standing about him, making inquiry about his master.

I was disturbed this night by a parcel of roaring fellows, that came rumbling upstairs to go to bed in the next room. They beat the walls with their elbows, as if they had a mind to batter down the house, being inspired, I suppose, by the great god Bacchus. A certain horse–jockey in the company had a voice as strong as a trumpet, and Stentorlike he made the house ring. "Damn me," says he, "if you or any man shall have the jade for 100 pounds.

The jade is as good a jade as ever wore curb." (It is customary here to call both horses and mares by the name of *jades.*) I wished him and his jade both once and again at the devil for disturbing my rest, for, just as I was a–dropping asleep again he uttered some impertinence with his Stentorian voice, which made me start and waked me. My rest was broken all that night, and waking suddenly from a confused dream about my horse dropping dead under me in the road, I imagined I heard somebody breathe very high in the bed by me. I thought perhaps that my friend Stentor had thought fit to come there, and felt about with my arms, but could discover nothing but the bed clothes, tho' the sound continued very distinct in my ears for about a minute after I was broad awake, and then it died away by degrees. This, with some people, would have procured the house a bad name of its being haunted with spirits.

STANFORD

Thursday, August 30th.–I left Norwalk at seven in the morning, and rid ten miles of stony road, crossing several brooks and rivulets that run into the Sound, till I came to Stanford. A little before I reached this town, from the top of a stony hill I had a large open view or prospect of the country westward. The greatest part of it seemed, as it were, covered with a white crust of stone, for the country here is exceedingly rocky, and the roads very rough, rather worse than Stonington. I breakfasted at Stanford at one Ebenezer Weak's. In this town I saw a new church, which is now a–building, the steeple of which was no sooner finished than it was all tore to pieces by lightning in a terrible thunder–storm that happened here upon the first day of August in the afternoon. I observed the rafters of the steeple split from top to bottom and the wooden pins or trunnels that fastened the joints half drawn out.

While I was at breakfast at Weak's, there came in a crazy old man, who complained much of the hardness of the times and of pains in his back and belly. "Lackaday for poor old Joseph!" said the landlady. A little after him came in one Captain Lyon, living at Rye Bridge. He wore an affected air of wisdom in his phiz, and pretended to be a very knowing man in the affairs of the world. He said he had travelled the whole world over in his fancy, and would fain have persuaded us that he understood the history of mankind completely.

Most of his knowledge was pedantry, being made up of commonplace sentences and trite proverbs. I asked him if I should have his company down the road. He replied that he would be glad to wait on me, but had an appointment to eat some roast pig with a neighbour of his, which would detain him till the afternoon. So I departed the town without him.

I rode a stony and hilly road to Horseneck, and overtook an old man who rid a sorrel mare, with a colt following her. He told me he was obliged to ride slow for fear of losing the colt, for sometimes the creature strayed behind, meeting with jades upon the way. He said he had been travelling the country for three weeks, visiting his children and grandchildren, who were settled for fifty miles round him. He told me he had had twenty–one sons and daughters, of whom nineteen were now alive, and fifteen of them married and had children; and yet he himself did not marry till twenty–seven years of age, and was now only seventy–two years old. This old man called in at a house about two miles from Horseneck, where he said there lived a friend of his. An old fellow with a mealy hat came to the door, and received him with a "How d'ye, old friend Jervis?" So I parted with my company.

HORSENECK

I passed thro' Horseneck, a scattered town, at half an hour after eleven o'clock, and passed over Rye Bridge at twelve, the boundary of Connecticut and York Government, after having rid 155 miles in Connecticut Government.

YORK GOVERNMENT

"Farewell, Connecticut" (said I, as I passed along the bridge), "I have had a surfeit of your ragged money, rough roads, and enthusiastick people." The countries of Connecticut and New England are very large and well peopled, and back in the country here, upon the navigable rivers, as well as in the maritime parts, are a great many fine large towns. The people here are chiefly husbandmen and farmers. The staples are the same as in the Massachusetts Province. They transport a good many horses to the West Indies, and there is one town in this Province that is famous for plantations of onions, of which they send quantities all over the continent and to the islands, loading sloops with them. Many of these onions I have seen nearly as large as a child's head.

It is reported that in Connecticut alone they can raise fifty or sixty thousand men able to bear arms. One Mr. Law' is present Governour of the Province. It is but a deputy Government under that of New England or the Massachusetts.'

Coming into York Government I found better)ads, but not such a complaisant people for salutig upon the road, tho' in their houses they are either so wild nor so awkward. It is to no pur)se here to ask how many miles it is to such a place. hey are not at all determined in the measure of ieir miles. Some will tell you that you are two files from your stage. Ride half a mile farther, they'll tell you it is four; a mile farther; you'll be told it is six miles, and three miles farther they'll say it is seven, and so on.

NEW ROCHELLE

I had a long ride before I arrived at New Rochelle, where I dined at the house of one Le Compte, a Frenchman, who has a daughter that is a sprightly, sensible girl.

KINGSBRIDGE

Coming from thence at four o'clock, I put up this night at Doughty's, who keeps house at Kingsbridge; a fat man, much troubled with the rheumatism, and of a hasty, passionate temper. I supped upon roasted oysters, while my landlord eat roasted ears of corn at another table. He kept the whole house in a stir to serve him, and yet could not be pleased.

This night proved very stormy and threatened rain. I was disturbed again in my rest by the noise of a heavy tread of a foot in the room above. That wherein I lay was so large and lofty that any noise echoed as if it had been in a church.

Friday, August 31st.–I breakfasted at Doughty's. My landlord put himself in a passion because his daughter was tardy in getting up to make my chocolate. He spoke so thick in his anger and in so sharp a key that I did not comprehend what he said.

I saw about fifty Indians fishing for oysters in the gut before the door. The wretches waded about stark naked, and threw the oysters as they picked them up with their hands into baskets that hung upon their left shoulders. They are a lazy, indolent generation, and would rather starve than work at any time, but being unacquainted with our luxury, Nature in them has few demands, which are easily satisfied.

YORK ISLAND

I passed over Kingsbridge at nine o'clock, and had a pleasant ride to York. This small island is called York Island from the City of York, which stands upon tile southwest end of it. It is a pleasant spot of ground, covered with several small groves of trees.

TURTLE BAY

About three miles before I reached York I saw the man–of–war commanded by Commodore Warren lying in Turtle Bay. This was a festival day with the crew. They were a–roasting an entire ox upon a wooden spit, and getting drunk as fast as they could, Warren having given them a treat. I was overtaken here by a young gentleman who gave me a whole packet of news about prizes and privateering, which is now the whole subject of discourse. I met one Dutchman on the road, who addressed me: "May I be so bold, where do you come from, sir?"

NEW YORK

I arrived in New York about eleven o'clock, and put up my horses at Waghorn's. After calling at Mrs. Hogg's, I went to see my old friend Todd, expecting there to dine, but accidentally I encountered Stephen Bayard, who carried me to dine at his brother's.

There was there a great company of gentlemen; among the rest Mr. D cie,' the Chief Justice, Mr. H–n, the City Recorder, and one Mr. More, a lawyer. There was one gentleman there whom they styled captain, who squinted the most abominably of anybody ever I saw. His eyes were not matched, for one was of a lighter colour than the other.

Another gentleman there wore so much of a haughty frown in his countenance, that even when he smiled it did not disappear. There were thirteen gentlemen at table, but not so much as one lady. We had an elegant, sumptuous dinner, with a fine dessert of sweetmeats and fruits, among which last there were some of the best white grapes I have seen in America.

The table chat ran upon privateering and such discourse as has now become so common that it is tiresome and flat. One there who set up for a dictator talked very much to the discredit of Old England, preferring New York to it in every respect whatsoever relating to good living. Most of his propositions were gratis dicta, and it seemed as if he either would not or did not know much of that fine country England. He said that the grapes there were good for nothing but to set a man's teeth on edge; but to my knowledge I have seen grapes in gentlemen's gardens there far preferable to any ever I saw in these northern parts of America. He asserted also that no good apple could be brought up there without a glass and artificial heat, which assertion was palpably false and glaringly ignorant, for almost every fool knows that apples grow best in northern climates betwixt the latitudes of thirty–five and fifty, and that in the southern hot climes, within the tropics, they don't grow at all, and therefore the best apples in the world grow in England and in the north of France. He went even so far as to say that the beef in New York was preferable to that of England. When he came there I gave him up as a trifler, and giving no more attention to his discourse, he lost himself, the Lord knows how or where, in a thicket of erroneous and ignorant dogmas, which any the most exaggerating traveller would have been ashamed of.

But he was a great person in the place, and therefore none in the company was imprudent enough to contradict him, tho' some were there that knew better.

I have known in my time some of these great dons take upon them to talk in an extravagant and absurd manner: "What a fine temperate climate this is!" says a certain dictating fop, while everybody that hears him is conscious that it is fit for none but the devil to live in. "Don't you think them fine oysters," says another exalted prig, while everybody knows he is eating of eggs. This we cannot conceive proceeds from ignorance, but from a certain odd pleasure they have in talking nonsense without being contradicted. This disposition may arise from the natural perverseness of human nature, which is always most absurd and unreasonable when free from curb or restraint. This company after dinner sent in for bumpers, so I left them at three o'clock.

I heard this day that Mr. H–l was in town, and that Ting, master of the Boston galley, had taken Morpang, the French cruiser, after a desperate battle and the loss of many men; but to this I gave little credit. By letters from Lisbon we had an account of Admiral Matthews having taken eighty French trading ships up the straits.

Saturday, September ist.–I breakfasted with Mrs. Hogg this morning, and at breakfast there was a good number of gentlemen; among the rest one Mr. Griffith from Rhode Island in five days, who informed us that the news of Morpang's being taken was a fiction. I called at Mr. Bayard's in the morning, but found him not at home. I met my old friend Dr. McGraa at the door, who told me he had seen Mr. H–11, and that he had expressed a desire of seeing me. I dined at Todd's with a mixed company, and in the afternoon crossed the river to Baker's in company with Dr. Colchoun and another gentleman. We stayed and drank some punch there, and viewed the French prizes in the harbour.

We returned to town at seven o'clock. We went to the Hungarian Club at night, where were present the Chief Justice, the City Recorder, Mr. Philips,' the Speaker of the House of Assembly, and several others. We had a deal of news by the Boston papers and some private letters, and among other news, that of the Dutch having declared war against France, and the capture of some of the barrier towns in Flanders by the French, as also the taking of some tobacco ships near the capes of Virginia, which furnished matter for conversation all night. We had an elegant supper, and among other things an excellent dish of young green pease. I wanted much to have met with H–11 this day, but heard that he was gone over to Long Island.

Sunday, September 2d.–I stayed at home the forenoon, and dined with Stephen Bayard. Just as we had done dinner, we heard two raps at the door solemnly laid on with a knocker. A gentleman in the company was going to see who it was, but Mr. Bayard desired him not to trouble himself, for it was only the *domper*. I asked who that was. He told me it was a fellow that made a course thro' one quarter of the town, giving two raps at each door as he passed to let the people in the houses know that the second bell had rung out. This man has a gratuity f rom each f amity for so doing every new year. His address, when he comes to ask for his perquisite, is: "Sir" or "Madam, you know what Imean." So he receives a piece of money, more or less, according to pleasure. This custom first began in New York, when they had but one bell to warn the people to church, and that bell happened to be cracked, so, for the sake of lucre, the sextons have kept it tip ever since. Such a trifling office as this perhaps is worth about forty pounds a year York currency, tho' the poor fellow sometimes is drubbed for his trouble by newcomers who do not understand the custom.

After dinner Mr. Jeffrys came in, and we had some very comical jaw. He spoke of going to Maryland along with me. I went home at four o'clock and supped this night with Mr. Hogg, there being a Scots gentleman in company. Just before supper Mr. Bourdillon came in, at the sight of whom we were all surprised, he having been a pretty while gone from these parts. He gave us an account of his adventures, and the misfortunes he had met with since his departure, of his narrowly escaping a drowning in his voyage to Curaçao, his being taken by the Spaniards in his passage from Jamaica to New York, and the difficulties and hardships he went thro' in making his escape, being obliged to live for four days upon nothing but a quart of water, and being driven out to the open ocean in a small undecked boat till he was providentially taken up by a Philadelphia sloop, bound homewards to Philadelphia.

Monday, September 3d.–I stayed at home all this forenoon, and dined at Todd's, where was a very large company, and among the rest Mr. Bourdillon, who told us that he had seen our quondam acquaintance Paul Ruiz among his countrymen the Spaniards. In the afternoon I went to the coffeehouse and read the newspapers, and coming home at six o'clock, I drank some punch with Mr. Hogg and one Heath, a dry old chap.

Tuesday, September 4th.–This day proving very rainy, I kept my room the greatest part of it. I dined with Mr. Hogg and family, and after dinner the discourse turned upon hystericks and vapours in women, when Mr. Hogg, pretending to discover to me an infallible cure for these distempers spoke good neat bawdy before his wife, who did not seem to be much surprised at it. He told me that a good mowing was a cure for such complaints. I concluded that this kind of talk was what his wife had been used to, but it is an inexcusable piece of rudeness and rusticity in the company of women to speak in this manner, especially when it is practised before wives and daughters, whose ears should never receive anything from husbands and fathers but what is quite modest and clean.

In the afternoon I sauntered about some time in the coffee–house, where were some rattling fellows playing at backgammon, and some deeper headed politicians at the game of chess. At six I went home, and, meeting with Mr. Bourdillon, he and I went to Todd's together, expecting to sup and have some chat snugly by ourselves, but we were interrupted by three young rakes who bounced in upon us, and then the conversation turned from a grave to a wanton strain. There was nothing talked of but ladies and lovers, and a good deal of polite smut. We drank two remarkable toasts, which I never before heard mentioned: the first was to our dear selves, and the tenour of the other was my own health. I told them that if such ridiculous toasts should be heard of out of doors, we should procure the name of the Selfish Club. We supped and dismissed at nine o'clock. Mr. Bourdillon and I went home like two philosophers, and the others went a–whoring like three rakes.

Wednesday, September 5th.–It threatened rain all day, and I did not go much abroad. I went in the morning with Mr. Hogg to the Jews' synagogue,' where was an assembly of about fifty of the seed of Abraham, chanting and singing their doleful hymns round the sanctuary (where was contained the ark of the covenant and Aaron's rod), dressed in robes of white silk. They had four great wax candles lighted, as large as a man's arm. Before the rabbi, who was elevated above the rest in a kind of desk, stood the seven golden candlesticks, transformed into silver gilt. They were all slip–shod. The men wore their hats in the synagogue, and had a veil of some white stuff, which they sometimes threw over their heads in their devotion; the women, of whom some were very pretty, stood up in a gallery like a hen–coop. They sometimes paused or rested a little from singing, and talked about business. My ears were so filled with their lugubrious songs that I could not get the sound out of my head all day.

I dined at Todd's with several gentlemen, and at night after playing a hit at backgammon with Mr. Hogg, I went to Todd's again with Mr. Bourdillon, where we supped by ourselves. It rained very hard, and we returned home at eleven o'clock at night.

Thursday, September 6th.–This day, the weather being somewhat more serene, I went more abroad, but it passed away, as many of our days do, unremarked and trifling. I did little more than breakfast, dine, and sup. I read some of Homer's twelfth Iliad, and went to the coffee–house in the afternoon, where I met my old friend Mr. Knockson, in whose vessel. I had made my voyage to Albany. I also saw there the learned Dr. McGraa, who told me for news that the Indians had already begun their hostilities by murdering some families of the back inhabitants. I played at backgammon with Mr. Hogg at night and supped with him.

Friday, September 7th.–This morning I had a visit from my tailor, who fitted me with a new coat and breeches, my clothes with which I set out being quite wore to a cobweb. Going to the coffee–house with Mr. Bourdillon at eleven o'clock, I played at backgammon with him and lost one hit. just as we had done playing Mr. H–11 came in, who saluted me and I him very cordially, and inquired of one another's welfare.

He told me he had been upon Long Island, and was very well, but only had got a broken head. "I hope," replied I, "you have not been a–fighting." "No," says he, "but I tumbled out of my chair." As I rid along the road there was another tall thin gentleman with him, who, by his visage jaune I took to be a West Indian, and I guessed right.

I dined at Todd's with Bourdillon and Dr. Colchoun. The doctor and I smoked a pipe after dinner and chopped politics. I went to Waghorn's at night to inquire of the state of my horses, and after having sat some time in a mixed company, Major Spratt came in, and he and I retired into a room by ourselves. He showed me a picture of a hermit in his cell, contemplating upon mortality with a death's–head in his hand. It was done in oil colours upon wood, and according to my judgment, it was a very nice piece of painting. About ten o'clock there came to us a drunken doctor, who was so intoxicated with liquor that he could scarce speak one connected sentence. He was much chagrined with some people for calling him a quack. "But God damn 'em," says he, "I have a case of pistols and sword; I'll make every blood of them own before long what it is to abuse a man of liberal education." I asked him what university he had studied at, Cambridge or Oxford. "Damn me, neither," said he. "Did you study at Leyden under Boerhaave, sir?" said I. "Boerhaave may go to hell for a fool and a blockhead as he was," said he, "that fellow was admired by all the world, and, damn his soul, I know not for what. For my part, I always had a mean opinion of him, only because he was one of them rascally Dutchmen, damn their souls." He went on at this rate for about half an hour. I, being tired of this kind of eloquence, left him to himself and went home.

Saturday, September 8th. –I called this morning at Mr. Bayard's, but he was not in town. I kept my nom most of the forenoon, and read Homer's thirenth Iliad. I dined at Todd's with a countryman mine, who had come from Virginia. He was a little ipper young fellow with a gaudy laced jacket; his ime Rhae, by trade a merchant, and had traveled most of the continent of English America. He mistook me for the doctor of the man–of–war, and, asking me when we should sail, I replied that I did not expect to sail anywhere till such time as I should cross the ferry.

We expected great news this night from Boston, having heard that some London ships had lately arrived there; but we were disappointed, for none had come. I supped at Todd's with Bourdillon and some French gentlemen. We heard news that Commodore Haynson in his way home had taken the Acapulco ship, a very rich prize, and that some ships from New York had been taken in their way home; but there are so many lies now stirring that I gave little credit to these *nouvelles.* This night was very sharp and cold. Bourdillon and I went home at eleven o'clock.

Sunday, September 9th.–I went this morning to the French church' with Mons. Bourdillon, and heard one Mons. Rue preach. He is reckoned a man of good learning and sense; but, being foolishly sarcastical, he has an unlucky knack at disobliging the best of his parishioners, so that the congregation has now dwindled to nothing.

I dined at Todd's with a mixed company, and had two letters: one from Dr. Moffatt at Rhode Island, in which I had the first news of the death of our great poet Pope, full of glory, tho' not of days; the other letter came from Boston, and came from the hand of La Moinnerie, which, for a specimen of the French compliment, I shall here transcribe:

A Boston, le 28me aoust 1744. MONSIEUR,–Je reçois dans ce moment, par Monsieur Hughes, la lettre que vous avez pris la peine de m'escrire, le 24 du courant, de Rhode Island, laquelle m'a fait un sensible plaisir, [en] apprenant votre heureuse arrivée en ce pays–là. Je désire que vous conserverez votre santé, et je redouble mes voeux à ciel pour que la fatigue du voyage ne vous soit point incommode. Vos nouvelles me prouvent entièrement la bonté que vous avez pour moi, et m'assurent aussi que j'avois tort de penser que mes entretiens vous incommodoient, car en vérité j'étois timide de vous arrêter si souvent et même dans les temps que vous étiez si souhaité dans ce qu'il y avoit de plus aimables compagnies, mais à vous parler franchement, je me trouvois si content avec vous que je fus aussi fort chagriné de votre départ, ainsi que tous vos amis l'ont été, et si mes affaires eussent pu finir, j'aurois été de votre compagnie jusque dans votre pays. Je tremble quand je fais réflexion sur l'hiver, si je suis obligé de rester dans les pays froids.

J'espère que vous me donnerez la satisfaction de m'escrire. Je tâcherai à la première de vous escrire en anglois, étant bien persuadé que vous voudriez bien excuser mon ignorance. Je me suis tant appliqué que j'ai conçu tous les mots de votre lettre, qui sont fort clairs et poétiques, et pour ne laisser aucune doute Monsieur le docteur Douglass m'a fait le plaisir de la lire.

Je n'ai pas encore pris ma médecine, mais je vais m'y déterminer.

Tous vos amis vous saluent et vous souhaitent bien de la santé. Je vous escris le présent par un docteur de médecine de la Barbade, qui va à Rhode Island. Je souhaite qu'il vous y trouve en bonne joie. Je suis parfaitement, monsieur et ami, votre très humble et très obéissant serviteur.

D. LA MOINNERIE, etc.
[Translation by William Gordon:]

[BOSTON, August 28, 1744. SIR,–I have this moment received, by Mr. Hughes, the letter which you have taken the trouble to write me of the 24th instant from Rhode Island. It has given me the greatest pleasure to learn of your safe arrival in that country. I sincerely trust that your health will be preserved and that the fatigues of the journey may not incommode you in the slightest degree.

What you say is to me a certain proof of your kindly regard, and convinces me that I was entirely wrong in supposing that my conversation disturbed you, for in truth I was afraid to intrude upon you so often and at times when you were so much desired and appreciated by the most amiable society. To confess the honest truth I was delighted with you and as grieved at your departure as any of your friends could have been, and if my affairs had permitted it would willingly have accompanied you into your own country. But I tremble when I think of winter if I should be compelled to make my abode in cold countries.

I am in hopes that you will give me the pleasure of hearing from you. I shall attempt for the first time to write in English, being quite certain that you will fully excuse my mistakes. I have studied very hard and I understand all the words in your letter, which were very clear and poetical, but so as to allow no doubt, Dr. Douglass did me the kindness to read it.

I have not yet taken my medicine, but am determined to do so. All your friends salute you and wish you abundant health. I write you this by a medical doctor of Barbadoes who is going to Rhode Island. Trusting that he will find you in the enjoyment of every happiness, I remain.

Dear sir and friend,

Your most humble and obedient servant,

(Signed) D. LA MOINNERIE, etc.]

I went this afternoon with Mr. Hogg to the Presbyterian meeting and heard there a good puritanick sermon preached by one Pemberton. I supped at Todd's with two or three of my countrymen, among whom was Mr. Knox.

Monday, September 10th.–I dined this day with Mr. Bayard's brother, and, after dinner, we tossed about the bumpers so furiously that I was obliged to go home and sleep for three hours and be worse than my word to Mr. H–ll, with whom I had promised to spend the evening. I writ to Dr. Moffatt at Newport, and to La Moinnerie at Boston, of which letter follows the copy :

A New York, le Lome de Septembre. Monsieur,–L'honneur de la vôtre, en date du 28me aoust, m'est bien parvenu. Je suis bien charmé que vous jouissiez d'une bonne santé, et vous remercie de la faveur que vous m'avez faite en m'escrivant. Pour ce qui me regarde, je jouis d'une parfaite santé depuis que j'ai laissé Boston. La seule chose que je regrette est de me voir séparé (et peut–être pour toujours) des agréables personnes avec qui je me suis rencontré et lié connaissance lors que j'étois à Boston, et en particulier de vous, monsieur, de qui l'humeur facétieuse, gaie, et la conversation agréable, me plaisoit beaucoup; mais, hélas! nos joies ne sont pas durables. Elles sont comme les nuages d'une belle soirée,–le soleil couchant, de différentes formes et de diverses couleurs charmantes; mais sitost que cette lumière glorieuse s'éloignera de notre horizon, et se couchera dans le sein de Thétis, sa belle maîtresse, ce spectacle brillant se dissipera, nous sommes dans le crépuscule, la nuit s'approche, il fait sombre! Hé bien, que pensez–vous, monsieur? sans doute que je soie devenu fou ou poète, escrivant de telles bagatelles dans une langue dont je n'entends pas le propre idiome, mais je me flatte que vous veuillez bien excuser mon ignorance.

J'ai vu de différents climats et de différents visages depuis que je vous ai quitté. A l'égard du pays, il est quelquefois montagneux et plein de roches, quelquefois c'est un terrain égal, et assez agréable. J'ai vu bien des hommes que l'on peut bien appeler fous, et d'autres gens d'esprit, mais j'en ai peu rencontré de sages. A l'égard du sexe, j'en ai vu dont les charmes seroient capables d'eschauffer les roches, ou de fondre des montagnes de glace.

Vraiment, monsieur, vous ne devez pas craindre l'hiver à Boston, puisque le sexe y est si plein de charmes et de chaleurs bénignes, mais je nen dis pas d'avantage, laissant à ceux qui en sont spectateurs, et qui sont du sang plus chaud que st le mien, les soins de les captiver.

You 'll pardon me, sir, for writing you in bad –ench. To make amends I subjoin a scrap of iglish, tho' not much better, yet I hope more operly expressed. I expect still to hear from u, and wish you all the health and tranquillity rich a mortal man can possibly enjoy. [Translation by William Gordon:

[New York, September. Sir –I have duly received your favour of the 28th August. I am delighted to learn that you are in the enjoyment of good health, and thank you for the honour you have done me in writing to me. With regard to myself I have enjoyed perfect health since I'left Boston. The only thing I regret is to find myself separated (and perhaps forever) from the agreeable persons I met and whose acquaintance I made while I was in Boston; and to you, sir, does this remark particularly refer, with whose gay facetious humour and pleasant conversation I was so greatly pleased. But, alas! our joys are transient. Like the clouds of a lovely evening at sunset, they assume different forms and divers charming colours, but as soon as the glorious luminary of day sinks beneath the horizon and goes to rest in the bosom of Thetis, his beautiful mistress, the glorious spectacle vanishes: we are in the twilight–night comes on apace–it is dark. Ah ! but what must you think, sir? certainly that I have either become a lunatic or a poet, to write such bagatelles in a language of which I don't even understand the correct idiom; I flatter myself, however, that you will kindly excuse my ignorance.

Since leaving you I have experienced different climates and have seen different faces. With respect to the country, it is sometimes mountainous and full of precipices, sometimes it is a level plain and very pleasant. I have seen many men whom one might well term fools, and met some wits, but few who could be deemed wise. Apropos of the sex, I have seen those whose charms would warm rocks, would melt icy mountains. Truly, sir, you have no need to fear the winter in Boston, since the sex there is so replete with charms and benignant warmth; but I will say no more, leaving to those who behold them and are of warmer blood than I the labour of captivating them.]

I supped at Todd's this night with a mixed company, where we had a deal of trifling chat.

Tuesday, September 11th.–This morning at the coffee–house I took my leave of Mr. H–1, who gave me his good wishes, and promised to write to me from Barbadoes.

FERRY- ELIZABETHTOWN POINT

I dined with my countryman, Mr. Rhea, at Mr. Bayard's, and, taking my leave of Mrs. Hogg and her sister after dinner, I took boat along with Mr. Rhea from York to Elizabethtown Point, and had a pleasant passage, making fifteen miles by water in three hours.

JERSEY GOVERNMENT- ELIZABETH TOWNWOODBRIDGE

MR. Rhea and I mounted horse, and rid twelve miles farther after sundown. We passed thro' Elizabethtown at seven o'clock at night, and arrived at Woodbridge at half an hour after eight. The country here is pleasant and pretty clear, with a beautiful intermixture of woods. The roads are very good in dry weather.

We put up at one Heard's, where we supped with a simple fellow, that had been bred up among the reeds and sedges, and did not seem as if ever he had conversed with men. His name was Mason, a Quaker by profession. Our landlady was a jolly fat woman, weighing about two hundredweight of fat.

I was sorry to leave New York, upon account of being separated from some agreeable acquaintance I had contracted there, and at the same time I cannot but own that I was glad to remove from a place where the temptation of drinking (a thing so incompatible with my limber constitution) threw itself so often in my way. I knew here several men of sense, ingenuity, and learning, and a much greater number of fops, whom I chuse not to name, not so much for fear of giving offence as because I think their names are not worthy to be recorded either in manuscript or printed journals. These dons commonly held their heads higher than the rest of mankind, and imagined few or none were their equals. But this I found always proceeded from their narrow notions, ignorance of the world, and low extraction, which indeed is the case with most of our aggrandized upstarts in these infant countries of America, who never had an opportunity to see, or (if they had) the capacity to observe the different ranks of men in polite nations, or to know what it is that really constitutes that difference of degrees.

Wednesday, September 12th.–I was waked this morning before sunrise with a strange bawling and hollowing without doors. It was the landlord ordering his negroes, with an imperious and exalted voice. In his orders the known term or epithet of *son of a bitch* was often repeated

I came downstairs, and found one Mr. White, a Philadelphian, and the loggerheaded fellow that supped with us last night ordering some tea for breakfast. Mr. Mason, among other judicious questions, asked me how cheeses sold in Maryland. I told him I understood nothing of that kind of merchandise, but if he wanted to know the price of cathartics and emetics there, I could inform him. He asked me what sort of commodities these were. I replied that it was a particular kind of truck which I dealt in. When our tea was made it was such abominable stuff that I could not drink of it, but drank a porringer of milk.

PITSCATUAY

We set off att seven o'clock and before nine passed thro' a place called Pitscatuay about 3 miles from Brunswick. I have observed that severall places upon the American main go by that name. The country here is pleasant and levell, intermixed with skirts of woods and meadow ground, the road in generall good but stormy in some places.

RARITAN FERRY–BRUNSWICK

We crossed Raretin River and arrived in Brunswick att 9 o'clock. We baited our horses and drank some chocolate at Miller's.

KINGSTON

We mounted again at ten, and after riding fifteen miles of a pleasant road, the day being somewhat sultry, we put up at Leonard's at Kingston, a little before one, where we dined. Here we met with an old chattering fellow, who imagined that Mr. Rhea was an officer of Warren's man–of–war, and wanted to list himself. He told us he had served in Queen Anne's wars, and that he was born under the Crown :)f England, and that eighteen years ago he had left the service, and lived with his wife.

We asked him where his wife was now. He answered he supposed in hell, "asking your honour's pardon, for she was such a plague that she was fit for nobody's company but the devil's." We could scarcely get rid of this fellow, till we made him so drunk with rum that he could not walk. He drank to Captain Warren's health, and subjoined, "not forgetting King George." We took horse again at three o'clock, and White and the Quaker kept in close conversation upon the road, about twenty paces before, while Rhea and I held a conference by ourselves.

MAIDENHEAD–TRENTON

At five o'clock we passed thro' a town called Maidenhead, and at six arrived at Bond's in Trenton, where we put up for all,night. Here Mason, the Quaker, left us, little regretted, because his company was but insipid. Just as Rhea and I lighted at the door, there came up a storm at northwest, which we were thankful we had so narrowly escaped, for it blowed and rained vehemently.

We had Dr. Cadwaller's company at supper and that of another gentleman in town, whose name I cannot remember. There passed a great deal of physical discourse betwixt the doctor and me, of which Rhea and White being tired went to bed, and I followed at eleven o'clock.

DELAWARE FERRY

Thursday, September 13th.–This morning proved very sharp and cold. We set out from Trenton at seven o'clock, and, riding thro' a pleasant road, we crossed Delaware Ferry a little before eight, where the tide and wind being both strong against us, we were carried a great way down the river before we could land.

BRISTOL

We arrived at Bristo' betwixt nine and ten o'clock, and breakfasted at Walton's.

SHAMMANY FERRY

Setting out from thence we crossed Shammany Ferry at eleven o'clock. The sun growing somewhat warmer we travelled with ease and pleasure. We stopped some time at a house within thirteen miles of Philadelphia, where there was an overgrown landlady much of the size of B–y M–t at Annapolis, who gave us bread and cheese and some cold apple–pie, but we paid dear for it.

Before we went into town, we stopped to see the works, where they were casting of cannon, where I thought they made but bungling work of it, spoiling ten where they made one.

PHILADELPHIA

We entered Philadelphia at four o'clock and Rhea and I put up at Cockburn's.' I went at six o'clock and spent the evening with Collector Alexander.

Friday, September 14th.–I stayed at home most of the forenoon, the air being somewhat sharp and cold. I dined with Mr. Currie and Mr. Weemse, at a private house, and, going home after dinner, read one of Shakespear's plays. I drank tea with my landlady Mrs. Cume, and at five o'clock went to the coffee–house, where I saw Dr. Spencer, who for some time had held a course of physical lectures of the experimental kind here and at New York. I delivered him a letter from Dr. Moffatt at Newport. I met here likewise one Mitchell, a practitioner of physick in Virginia, who was travelling as he told me upon account of his health. He was a man much of my own make, and his complaints were near akin to mine. Here I met Dr. Phineas Bond and others of my old acquaintances.

At Philadelphia I heard news of some conturbations and fermentations of parties at Annapolis, concerning the election of certain parliament members for that wretched city, and was sorry to find that these trifles still contributed so much to set them at variance, but I pray that the Lord may pity them, and not leave them entirely to themselves and the devil. I went home at eight at night, the air being cold and raw, and was sorry to hear that my fellow traveller Mr. Rhea was taken with an ague, the effect of our night's ride upon Tuesday.

Saturday, September 25th.–This morning proving rainy, I stayed at home till eleven o'clock, at which time my barber came to shave me, and gave me a harangue of politics and news. I paid a visit to Dr. Thomas Bond, and went and dined at Cockburn's in company with two stanch Quakers, who sat at table with their broad hats upon their heads. They eat a great deal more than they spoke, and their conversation was only yea and nay. In the afternoon I had a visit of Mr. Rhea, who had expelled his ague by the force of a vomit.

At six o'clock I went to the coffee–house and thence with Mr. Alexander to the Governour's club, where the Governour himself was present, and several other gentlemen of note in the place. The conversation was agreeable and instructing, only now and then some persons there showed a particular fondness for introducing gross, smutty expressions, which I thought did not altogether become a company of philosophers and men of sense.

Sunday, September 16th.–This morning proved very sharp, and it seemed to freeze a little. I breakfasted at Neilson's with Messrs. Home and Watts and went to the Presbyterian meeting in the morning with Mr. Wallace. There I heard a very Calvinistical sermon preached by an old holderforth, whose voice was somewhat rusty, and his countenance a little upon the four square. The pulpit appeared to me somewhat in shape like a tub, and at each side of it aloft was hung an old–fashioned brass sconce.

In this assembly was a collection of the most curious old–fashioned screwed–up faces, both of men and women, that ever I saw. There were a great many men in the meeting with linen nightcaps, an indecent and unbecoming dress, which is too much wore in all the churches and meetings in America that I have been in, unless it be those of Boston, where they are more decent and polite in their dress, tho' more fantastical in their doctrines, and much alike in their honesty and morals.

I dined with Collector Alexander, and in the afternoon went with Mr. Weemse to the Roman Chapel, where I heard some fine musick and saw some pretty ladies. The priest, after saying mass, catechized some children in English, and insisted much upon our submitting our reason to religion and believing of everything that God said (or properly speaking everything that the priest says, who often has the impudence to quote the divine authority to support his absurdities), however contradictory or repugnant it seemed to our natural reason. I was taken with a sick qualm in this chapel, which I attributed to the gross nonsense, proceeding from the mouth of the priest, which, I suppose, being indigestible bred crudities in my intellectual stomach, and confused my animal spirits. I spent the evening at the tavern with some Scotsmen.

Monday, September 17th.–This day was very sharp and cold for the season, and a fire was very grateful. I did little but stay at home all day, and employed my time in reading of Homer's Iliad. I dined at the tavern, and walked out to the country after dinner to reap the benefit of the sharp air. When I returned I drank tea with Mrs. Cume, and there being some ladies there, the conversation ran still upon the old topic, religion.

I had a letter from my brother in Maryland, where there was an account of some changes that had happened there since I left the place. At the coffee–house I could observe no new faces, nor could I learn any news.

Tuesday, September 18th.–This forenoon I spent in reading of Shakespear's *Timon of Athens, or Manhater,* a play which, tho' not written according to Aristotle's rules, yet abounds with inimitable beauties, peculiar to this excellent author.

I dined at Cockburn's, where was a –set of very comical phizzes, and a very vulgar unfurbished conversation, which

I did not join in, but eat my dinner and was a hearer, reaping as much instruction from it as it would yield.

I paid a visit to Collector Alexander in the afternoon, and at night going to the coffee–house, I went from thence, along with Messrs. Wallace and Currie, to the Musick Club, where I heard a tolerable *concerto* performed by a harpsichord and three violins. One Levy there played a very good violin; one Quin bore another pretty good part; Tench Francis played a very indifferent finger upon an excellent violin, that once belonged to the late Ch. Calvert, Governour of Maryland. We dismissed at eleven o'clock, after having regaled ourselves with musick, and good viands and liquor.

Wednesday, September 19th.–To–day I resolved to take my departure from this town. In the morning my barber came to shave me and almost made me sick with his Irish brogue and stinking breath. He told me that he was very glad to see that I was after being of the right religion. I asked him how he came to know what religion I was of. "Ohon ! and sweet Jesus now!" said he, "as if I had not see your Honour at the Roman Catholic chapel, coming upon Sunday last." Then he ran out upon a blundering encomium concerning the Catholicks and their principles. I dined with Mr. Alexander, and, taking my leave of him and wife, I went to Mr. Strider's in Front Street, where I had some commissions to deliver to Mr. Tasker at Annapolis.

SKUYLKILL FERRY–DARBY

Taking horse at half an hour after three o'clock, I left Philadelphia, and crossed Skuylkill Ferry. At a quarter after four, I passed thro' the town of Darby about an hour before sunset.

CHESTER

About the time of the sun's going down, the air turned very sharp, it being a degree of frost. I arrived in Chester, about half an hour after seven, riding into town in company with an Irish Teague who overtook me on the road. Here I put up at one Mather's, an Irishman, at the sign of the Ship.

At my seeing of the city of Philadelphia, I conceived a quite different notion of both city and inhabitants from that which I had before from the account or description of others. I could not apprehend this city to be so very elegant or pretty as it is commonly represented. In its present situation it is much like one of our country market towns in England. When you are in it the majority of the buildings appear low and mean, the streets unpaved, and therefore full of rubbish and mire. It makes but an indifferent appearance at a distance, there being no turrets or steeples to set it off to advantage, but I believe that in a few years hence it will be a great and flourishing place, and the chief city in North America.

The people are much more polite, generally speaking, than I apprehended them to be from the common account of travellers. They have that accomplishment, peculiar to all our American Colonies; viz., subtlety and craft in their dealings. They apply themselves strenuously to business, having little or no turn towards gayety (and I know not indeed how they should, since there are few people here of independent fortunes or of high luxurious taste). Drinking here is not at all in vogue, and in the place there is pretty good company and conversation to be had. It is a degree politer than New York, tho' in its fabriek not so urbane, but Boston excels both for politeness and urbanity, tho' only a town.

Thursday, September 20th.–I set out at nine o'clock from Mather's and about two miles from Chester was overtaken by a Quaker, one of the politest and best behaved of that kidney ever I had met with. We had a deal of discourse about news and politicks, and after riding four miles together we parted.

I now entered the confines of the three–notched road, by which I knew I was near Maryland. Immediately upon this something ominous happened, which was my man's tumbling down, plump, two or three times, horse and baggage and all, in the middle of a plain road. I, likewise, could not help thinking that my state of health was changed for the worse upon it.

WILMINGTON

Within a mile of Wilmington I met Mr. Neilson of Philadelphia, who told me some little scraps of news from Annapolis.

CHRISTIN FERRY–NEWCASTLE

I crossed Christin Ferry at twelve o'clock, and at two o'clock I dined at Griffith's in Newcastle, and had some chat with a certain virtuoso of the town who came in after dinner. I departed thence at half an hour after three, and about a mile from town I met a monstrous appearance, by much the greatest wonder and prodigy I had seen in my travels, and every whit as strange a sight by land as a mermaid is at sea. It was a carter driving his cart along the road, who seemed to be half man, half woman. All above from the crown of his head to the girdle seemed quite masculine, the creature having a great hideous unshorn black beard and strong coarse features, a slouch hat, cloth jacket, and great brawny fists, but below the girdle there was nothing to be seen but petticoats, a white apron, and the exact shape of a woman with relation to broad round buttocks. I would have given something to have seen this creature turned topsy–turvy, to have known whether or not it was an hermaphrodite, having often heard of such animals, but never having seen any to my knowledge; but I thought it most prudent to pass by peaceably, asking no questions, lest it should prove the devil in disguise.

Some miles farther I met two handsome country girls, and inquired the road of them. One seemed fearful, and the other was very forward and brisk. I liked the humour and vivacity of the latter, and lighted from my horse as if I had been going to salute her; but they both set up a scream and ran off like wild bucks into the woods.

I stopped this night at one Van Bibber's, a house twelve miles from Newcastle. The landlady here affected to be a great wit, but the landlord was a heavy lubber of Dutch pedigree. The woman pretended to be jealous of her husband with two ugly old maids that were there; one of whom was named Margaret, who told me she was born in Dundee in Scotland, and asked me if ever I had drunk my Dundee *swats out o f twa–lugged bickers*. (Ale out of two–eared cups.) These two old maids would sit, one at each side of Van Bibber and tease him, while his wife pretended to scold all the time, as if she was jealous, and he would look like a goose.

There were in this house a certain Irish Teague, and one Gilpin, a dweller in Maryland. The Teague and Gilpin lay in one bed upon the floor, and I in a lofty bedstead by myself. Gilpin and I talked over politicks and news relating to Maryland, while we were in bed, before we went to sleep, and our discourse was interlaced with hideous yawnings, like two tired and weary travellers, till at last the nodding deity took hold of us in the middle of half–uttered words and broken sentences. My rest was broken and interrupted, for the Teague made a hideous noise in coming to bed, and as he tossed and turned kept still ejaculating either an *ohon* or *sweet Jesus.*

*Fridav, September 21st–*I was waked early this morning by the groanings, *ohous*, and yawnings of our Teague, who every now and then gaped fearfully, bawling out, "O sweet Jesus!" in a mournful, melodious accent; in short he made as much noise between sleeping and waking as half a dozen hogs in a little pen could have done; but Mr. Gilpin, his bedfellow, was started and gone.

MARYLAND–BOHEMIA

I took horse at nine o'clock, and arrived at Bohemia at twelve. I called at the manor–house, and dined there with Miss Coursey. She and I went in the afternoon to visit Colonel Colville,' and returned home betwixt eight and nine at night. 653.

Saturday, September 22d.– I rid this morning with Miss Coursey to visit Bouchelle, the famous Yaw doctor, who desired me to come and prescribe for his wife, who had got an hysterick palpitation, or as they called it *a wolf in her heart.* I stayed and dined with him, and there passed a deal of conversation between us. I found the man much more knowing than I expected from the common character I had heard of him. He seemed to me a modest young fellow, not insensible of his depth in physical literature, neither quite deficient in natural sense and parts. His wife having desired my advice I gave it, and was thanked by the husband and herself for the favour of my visit.

There was there an old comical fellow named Millner, who went by the name of *doctor*. He was busy making a pan of melilot plaster, and seemed to have a great conceit of his own learning. He gave us a history of one Du Witt, a doctor at Philadelphia, who he said had begun the world in the honourable station of a porter, and used to drive a turnip cart or wheelbarrow thro' the streets. This old fellow was very inquisitive with me, but I did not incline much to satisfy his curiosity. He asked me if Miss Coursey was my wife. After dinner we returned homewards.

Sunday, September 23d.–There came up a furious northwest wind this morning, which prevented my setting off, as I intended, knowing that I could not cross the ferries. I was shaved by an Irish barber, whose hand was so heavy that he had almost flayed my chin and head. Miss Coursey and I dined by ourselves, and at four o'clock we walked to Colonel Colville's, where we spent the evening agreeably, and returned home at eight o'clock, the night being cold and blustering and the wind in our teeth.

Monday, September 24th.–It seemed to threaten to blow hard this morning, but the wind changing to south before twelve o'clock, it began to moderate and I had hopes of getting over Elk Ferry. I dined with Miss Coursey at Colonel Colville's, and set out from there at three o'clock, intending at night for Northeast.

On the road here, at one Altum's, who keeps publick house at Elk Ferry, I met with my Irish barber, who had operated upon my chin at Bohemia, who had almost surfeited me with his palaver. I had some learned conversation with my ingenious friend Terence, the ferry–man, and as we went along the road, the barber would fain have persuaded me to go to Parson Wye's to stay that night, which I refused, and so we took leave of one another.

I went the rest of the way in the company of a man who told me he was a carter, a horse–jockey, a farmer,–all three. He asked me if I had heard anything of the wars in my travels, and told me he heard that the Queen of Sheba, or some such other queen, had sent a great assistance to the King of England, and that if all was true that was said of it, they would certainly kill all the French and Spaniards before Christmas next.

NORTHEAST

Talking of these matters with this unfinished politician, I arrived at Northeast at seven o'clock at night, and put up at one Smith's there. After supper I overheard a parcel of superficial philosophers in the kitchen, talking of knotty points in religion over a mug of cider. One chap, among the rest, seemed to confound the whole company with a show of learning, which was nothing but a puff of clownish pedantry. I went to bed at ten o'clock.

SUSQUEHANNA FERRY

Tuesday, September 25th.–I departed Northeast this morning at nine o'clock. The sky was dark and cloudy, threatening rain. I had a solitary ride over an unequal, gravelly road till I came to Susquehanna Ferry, where I baited my horses, and had a ready passage, but was taken with a vapourish qualm in the ferry–boat, which went off after two or three miles' riding–I dined art my old friend Tradaway's, whom I found very much indisposed with fevers. He told me it had been a very unhealthy time and a hot summer. I should have known the time had been unhealthy without his telling me so, by only observing the washed countenances of the people standing at their doors, and looking out at their windows, for they looked like so many staring ghosts. In short I was sensible I had got into Maryland, for every house was an infirmary, according to ancient custom.

JOPPA

I arrived at Joppa at half an hour after five o'clock, and putting up at Brown's, I went and paid a visit to the parson and his wife, who were both complaining, or grunting (as the country phrase is), and had undergone the penance of this blessed climate, having been harassed with fevers ever since the beginning of August. I took my leave of them at eight o'clock, and supped with my landlord.

GUNPOWDER FERRY–NEWTOWN

Wednesday, September 26th.–This morning proved very sharp and cool. I got over Gunpowder Ferry by ten o'clock, and rid solitary to Newtown upon Patapscoe, where I dined at Rogers's and saw some of my acquaintances.

PATAPSCOE FERRY

I crossed Patapscoe Ferry at four o'clock, and went to Mr. Hart's, where I stayed that night. We talked over old stories, and held a conference some time with a certain old midwife there, one Mrs. Harrison, and having finished our consultations, we went to bed at ten o'clock. 664.

Thursday, September 27th.–I set off from Mr. Hart's a little after nine o'clock, and baited at More's, where I met with some patients that welcomed me on my return.

ANNAPOLIS

I arrived at Annapolis at two o'clock afternoon, and so ended my peregrinations.

In these my northern travels I compassed my design, in obtaining a better state of health, which was the purpose of my journey. I found but little difference in the manners and character of the people in the different Provinces I passed thro' ; but as to constitutions and complexions, air and government, I found some variety. Their forms of government in the northern Provinces I look upon to be much better and happier than ours, which is a poor, sickly, convulsed State. Their air and living to the northward is likewise much preferable, and the people of a more gigantick size and make. At Albany, indeed, they are entirely Dutch, and have a method of living something differing from the English.

In this itineration I compleated, by land and water together, a course of 1624 miles. The northern parts I found in general much better settled in the southern. As to politeness and humanity they are much alike, except in the great towns, where the inhabitants are more civilized, especially at Boston.

Finis.

THE END.

~ * ~

Visit us at:

http://www.alejandroslibros.com

Publisher:

Alejandro's Libros © 2014

Other book you may like from America's Colonial Period.
Full Cover, paperback edition of the book entitled: "*A True History of the Captivity and Restoration of Mrs. Mary Rowlandson.*"

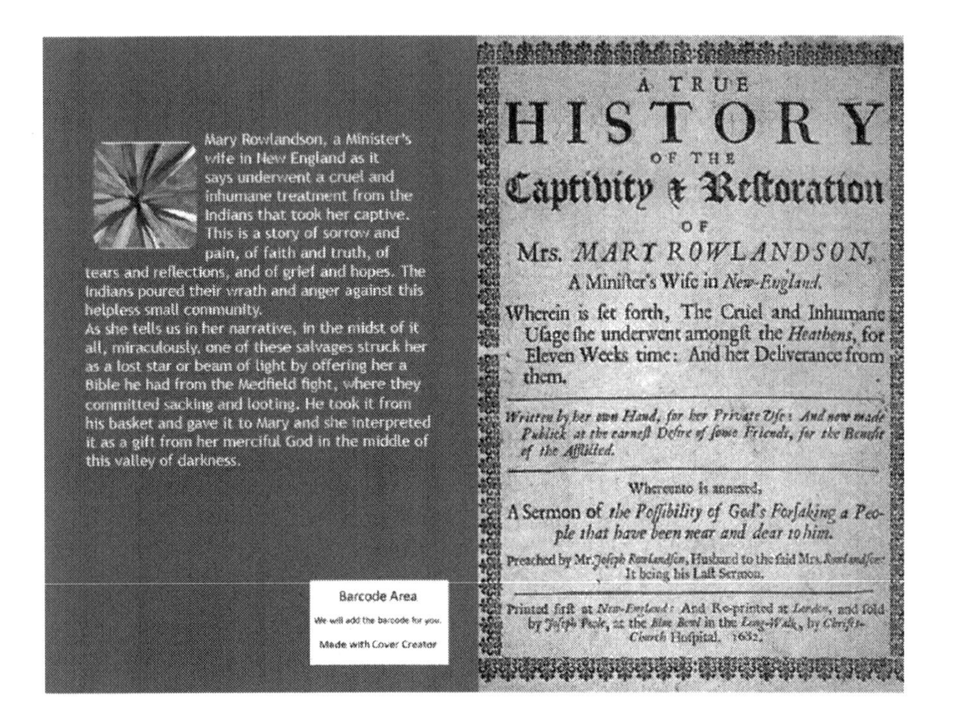

---

[i] Wendy Martin, *Colonial American Travel Narratives*. Penguin Books, 1994. *The Itinerarium of Dr. Alexander Hamilton,* p.175.

[ii] Ibid.179

[iii] Lecture.

[iv] Ibid.182.

[v] Lecture.

[vi] Ibid.191.

[vii] Ibid.204.

[viii] Ibid.220.

[ix] Ibid.240.

[x] Lecture.

[xi] Ibid.201.

[xii] Ibid.264.

[xiii] Lecture.

[xiv] Lecture.

Made in the USA
Middletown, DE
25 April 2017